CW01073135

STAFFORDSHIRE LIBRARY AND INFORMATION SERVICES
Please return or renew by the last date shown

STAFFORD LIBRARY
01785 278585

27 FEB 2011

26. MAY

01/10/15 +
13/10/15 +
16 JUN 2011

If not required by other readers, this item may be renewed in person, by post or telephone, online or by email.
To renew, either the book or ticket are required

24 HOUR RENEWAL LINE 0845 33 00 740

3 8014 07042 1448

Finding The Foe

Dedication

To Gefr Franz Becker I./KG 54

Missing 21 August 1940

Denied a known grave by circumstances and events

Finding The Foe

Outstanding Luftwaffe Mysteries of the Battle of Britain and Beyond Investigated and Solved

Andy Saunders

Grub Street • London

Published by
Grub Street Publishing
4 Rainham Close
London
SW11 6SS

Copyright © Grub Street 2010
Copyright text © Andy Saunders 2010

British Library Cataloguing in Publication Data

Saunders, Andy.
Finding the foe : outstanding Luftwaffe mysteries of the
Battle of Britain and beyond investigated and solved.
1. Germany. Luftwaffe – History. 2. World War, 1939-1945 –
Aerial operations, German. 3. Britain, Battle of, Great
Britain, 1940. 4. World War, 1939-1945 – Missing in
action – Germany.
I. Title
940.5'44'943'0922-dc22

ISBN-13: 9781906502850

All rights reserved. No part of this publication may be reproduced, stored in a retrieval system, or transmitted in any form or by any means electronic, mechanical, photocopying, recording, or otherwise, without the prior permission of the copyright owner.

Design by Roy Platten, Eclipse, Hemel Hempstead
roy.eclipse@btopenworld.com

Printed and bound by MPG Ltd, Bodmin, Cornwall

Grub Street Publishing uses only FSC
(Forest Stewardship Council) paper for its books

Contents

Foreword

AS A PILOT WHO flew with the 3rd Staffel ,of the German bomber group Kampfgeschwader 2 during 1940, I have special cause to take particular interest in the cases of my former comrades who flew operationally over Britain during the Second World War and who failed to return. Most particularly, I cannot help but be moved by the stories of those casualties who are still missing or who remain unidentified, some of which have touched me directly.

Heinz Möllenbrok.

On 16 August 1940 I was shot down in my Dornier 17 over north Kent and taken prisoner of war, very badly wounded, near a place called Staple. Two of my crew were killed. Not far away from my incident some other men from my same unit had also been shot down and killed that same day and are still listed as missing. Again, a few days before others from the unit were downed in the area and are still regarded as missing in action. I know that great efforts have been ongoing to try to have these men identified and this is work that has a great personal importance to me. But for the grace of God I could easily have been one of those men and I know how important it would have been to my family to have known what happened to me under those circumstances if I had been shot down and lost over a foreign country. As it was, I survived – but this only thanks to the great kindnesses shown to me by the British people, my enemies, during my captivity. From the very outset I was treated with humanity, dignity and compassion and I was given the very best medical treatment that saved both my life and my shattered arm. I was shown thoughtfulness and human kindness right up until the point that I was repatriated to Germany in 1943 due to my severe wounds. I have never forgotten this treatment, and I remain ever thankful for it. I came to attack these people and yet was shown compassion by those I had been sent to kill.

Whilst I knew none of the men personally who are detailed in this book, I am ever mindful of the fact that any one of them could so easily have been me. In fact, and by coincidence, the crew of a Messerschmitt 410 shot down near Eastbourne in 1943 and the crew of a Dornier 217 downed near Middlesbrough in the same year were both serving with my old unit, KG 2, when they died in action. Both crews are covered by my friend Andy Saunders in his fascinating book, and I was privileged to attend the burial of one of my KG 2 comrades from that Dornier 217 at a ceremony in England in 1998. During that visit I also met up with the English nurse who had looked after me with such dedicated care in 1940, a Mrs Sheila Bambridge. Andy had found her for me after so much patient research – incredibly living just a mile or so from his home in Sussex! It was a meeting that meant so much to me and I was able to reflect on my survival and what fate had decreed otherwise for my crew members and others like those of whom Andy Saunders writes here.

It has struck me that the kindness and humanity shown to me by the British in 1940 has continued to the present day through the impartial research work done by the people mentioned in this book many decades later in finding and identifying those who were lost. It was for that reason that I wrote a full report of Andy's good works to the German Embassy in London during 1996 and I was delighted that, as a result, Colonel Victor Zimmer was able to make a special award and commendation to the author of this book. Colonel Zimmer stated:

> "Thanks to your endeavours it has been possible to establish the names and fates of German aircrews and also to identify graves here in England. Through your books with their objective accounts you have also made a valuable contribution to German history and I take this opportunity to thank you for your valuable work and your contribution to Anglo-German reconciliation and friendship."

They are sentiments that I am delighted to echo in commending to you, the reader, this compelling and unique account that details missing German aircrews lost over Britain.

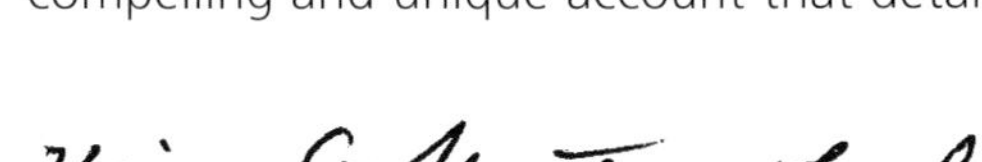

Heinz Möllenbrok
Former Leutnant of the German air force
Dornier 17 pilot, 3/KG 2
Prisoner of war 16 August 1940
(Sadly, Heinz Möllenbrok died when this book was in preparation)

Introduction

IN *FINDING THE FEW* (Grub Street 2009), which is my companion volume to this book, an account is given relating to the discovery of an RAF fighter pilot, Plt Officer George James Drake, who was found buried in the wreckage of his Hurricane at Goudhurst, Kent. Shot down during September 1940 he lay undiscovered until 1972 when he was found and identified by a private aircraft recovery group. Given the level of aerial activity in the wartime skies over southern England, especially during the Battle of Britain, and then the great flurry of aviation archaeology during the early 1970s it was inevitable that sooner or later the remains of hitherto 'missing' fliers of the Luftwaffe would also be found in the wreckage of their aircraft. Indeed, within a year of the discovery of George Drake the same team had found and recovered the wreck of a Messerschmitt 109 E-4 from deep beneath Kent's Romney Marsh. Entombed in the cockpit was its unfortunate pilot, Lt Werner Knittel.

Werner Knittel was not unique in being the only member of the Luftwaffe who remained unaccounted for after war flights over the British Isles and whilst it is just about impossible to put forward a total number of those aircrew from the Luftwaffe still missing from operations over British soil, it is certainly the case that such casualties who fall into this category must number into the many hundreds. Of these, some fell into coastal waters around Britain while many were buried in the UK as unidentified airmen. The disappearance of others might sometimes be explained by the catastrophic and total destruction of the aeroplane and its crew due to the explosion of bomb loads and fuel, and through the sheer force of impact into the ground. Sometimes, the ground happened to be so soft that it swallowed both plane and occupant whole. On other occasions it was ground so hard that almost total annihilation of the machine and any unfortunate occupant resulted.

In some cases there is clear evidence that remains *were* found at the crash scenes at the time and yet they were never afforded any form of proper burial. Those casualties certainly run into many dozens of known instances, and it was very often the case that remains were simply 'disposed' of in quite unceremonious ways. Sometimes, bodily remains were simply placed back into the crater caused by the crashing aircraft and covered over, or else they were unofficially buried nearby by the military, unmarked and unrecorded, often under adjacent hedges and trees. Such cases as these were sometimes due to the hostile reactions towards a much hated enemy and when such levels of disrespect for the enemy dead became, occasionally, an accepted norm. Feelings sometimes ran high – and at least in one case we will see that this persisted long after the war. On the other hand, great care was sometimes taken to find, identify and properly bury the enemy dead – affording them decently marked and cared for graves after elaborate burial ceremonies with full military honours. Indeed, and notwithstanding the feelings that had sometimes caused much lesser respect to be shown towards the enemy dead, such funerals invariably saw buglers, firing parties and coffins draped in swastika flags. This, of course, was an honour to war dead bestowed reciprocally by the Germans to allied casualties who fell in their territory. In fact, appropriate rites towards enemy war dead were laid down in the Geneva Convention in any event. Not only the rules for the general conduct of warfare or the treatment of prisoners were proscribed in the convention. The war dead were protected, too.

The cases covered in this book primarily involve those lost during the fighting of the Battle of Britain, although the sustained Luftwaffe air campaign against Britain right up until 1945 invariably saw many other missing casualties post-1940. Therefore, this book also examines many cases outside the 1940 period. Most of those covered here are casualties discovered during post-war excavations, although a number of the cases are instances where post-war research has allowed airmen previously buried as 'unknown' to be subsequently identified, headstones changed and families informed. Equally, there are other cases detailed where the mystery of that casualty's disappearance endures.

Whatever the cause for which these airmen fought and died they did so in the service of their country and were mourned by wives, girlfriends, siblings and parents. Drawing a line under some of these cases, even after such a long period of time, is as important a humanitarian task as is the closure given to many families of the hitherto missing RAF casualties who were covered in my previous book. By its very nature, the subject matter of this work portrays the grim reality of warfare and might make for sometimes uncomfortable reading, but the stories contained within it are put forward as an honest historical account of the loss of these men and their subsequent discovery or identification. Hopefully it will also stand as a memorial to some of these previously lost or missing airmen; servicemen whose ending can only be told because of the dedicated research carried out by very many private individuals or organisations. The importance and value of this work to those left behind, even after seventy years, is difficult to convey. Perhaps this book will serve to throw light on a sensitive topic as much as it will be a tribute to those who have sought to bring closure to the families of German aircrew.

NOTE: For the sake of clarity the term German War Graves Service is used throughout this book. The actual name of the organisation is the Volksbund Deutsche Kriegsgräberfürsorge e.V. (VDK)

Acknowledgements

MANY FRIENDS AND COLLEAGUES have greatly assisted me in writing this book. Without them this account detailing the stories behind missing Luftwaffe aircrew lost on operations over the British Isles would have been rather more difficult to put together.

I should like to thank, in no particular order of merit: Mark Kirby, Peter Cornwell, Chris Goss, Eddie Taylor, Dave Smith, Winston Ramsey, Martin O'Brien, Paul Cole, Steve Hall, Ian Hutton, Dennis Knight, Dean Sumner, Richard Hukins, Dave Buchanan, John Elgar-Whinney, Geoff Nutkins, Simon Parry, Philippa Hodgkiss, Gerry Burke, Jill Craig, Trevor Matthews, Danny Burt, Bjorn Rose and Adrian Crosson.

I must especially thank Philippa Hodgkiss for help that went way beyond the call of duty in sorting out and copying relevant file notes from the archives of our mutual late friend, Peter Foote. Her enthusiastic assistance was greatly appreciated and I would like to think that Peter, who had been so very closely involved in many of the cases covered in this volume, would have approved of the final result. He had been researching and recording details related to the subject matter of this book since the 1950s, and were it not for his ground-breaking work it is certain that much history would have otherwise been lost.

Without diminishing in any way my appreciation for the help of those listed above I feel that the biggest thank you of all must go to Joe Potter. Joe has involved himself over many years in the identification of previously unidentified Luftwaffe airmen buried in various cemeteries in the British Isles and the work he has done is astounding to say the very least. He was generous and enthusiastic to a fault in his support of this book project and gave freely of his time and knowledge. He was always ready to answer my queries, deal with e-mails on an almost daily basis, supply information or photographs and was generally a fund of useful knowledge. Again, he was one who went above and beyond the call of duty – particularly when he specially made a round-trip of some hundreds of miles to see me, armed with boxes of files, archives and photographs. Thank you, Joe.

Once more I must thank John Davies and his team at Grub Street, including Emer Hogan, Sophie Campbell and Sarah Driver. I look forward to working with you all again.

Last, but by no means least, a big thank you to Zoe who has again put up with my absence whilst I shut myself away in my study to prepare this manuscript. Your support and understanding has also gone above and beyond the call of duty! Thank you.

If I have overlooked anyone who has had an input to this book then I extend my sincerest apologies. It will have been entirely unintentional. Thank you again one and all.

CHAPTER 1

The Last of The Many?

WHEN DAVID BUCHANAN AND his team from the Brenzett Aeronautical Museum attended the military funeral of Plt Off George Drake, the young South African Hurricane pilot they had found in 1972, the authorities all but dismissed the find as a one-off. Indeed, the Ministry of Defence viewed as highly unlikely the chances of any other previously missing airmen from World War Two being found in the United Kingdom. Of course, they overlooked the fact that there were still scores of missing airmen missing from air operations over British soil. It also seemingly ignored the fact that so too were there many German airmen who had been lost in air operations against Britain and never found. Even the most cursory examination of, for example, RAF Intelligence reports detailing crashed enemy aircraft told its own story, and it was one such report that led David Buchanan and his Brenzett team to a Messerschmitt 109 crash site on Romney Marsh, Kent, and resulted in yet another formerly missing flier from the Battle of Britain being discovered – a little over nine months after George Drake had been laid to rest.

As a starting point for the Brenzett Aeronautical Museum's investigation, the RAF Intelligence report on the crash in the National Archives at Kew (the Public Record Office) contained sufficient information to steer the Brenzett team in the right direction, being specific about the aircraft type, the date and time of crash and its location:

> "Me 109. Crashed on 28 October 1940 at Fielding Land, Dymchurch. Map reference R.5549. Markings not decipherable but nose and tail from pieces of fabric found were yellow. Following fighter action aircraft dived into ground and is almost completely buried. From ammunition found the armament was probably two x 20mm shell guns and two MG17s. Pilot dead, buried in wreckage. No further details possible."

This information, coupled with contemporary eyewitness accounts brought to the museum by visitors, led the recovery group to suspect that an excavation of the site could well yield fruitful results although, of course, the question of the pilot and his fate was a matter that needed to be determined first. However, witness Jim Simson of St Mary's Bay had seen the aircraft coming down and was in no doubt that the pilot had never been taken out of the wreck. An infantry man home on embarkation leave, he recalled there was a scrap on and

Witness Jim Simson watched an air battle like this above Romney Marsh on 28 October 1940, as the Battle of Britain was drawing to its close. Out of the whirling specks and vapour trails high above, a Messerschmitt 109 came howling vertically down to plunge into the ground at Dymchurch. So violent was the impact with the soft ground that the German aircraft and its pilot were driven deep under the surface.

he could see little specks very high up in the sky. Suddenly, one of the aircraft started screaming down and as he was watching he saw a condensation 'halo' around the plummeting aircraft. It was the loudest noise he had ever heard an aircraft make and after it had thumped into the field the sound of the Messerschmitt could be heard following it down. At the crash site there was just a small hole with little pieces scattered around it, but as Simson had to return to his unit he didn't know what subsequently happened. However, when serving in Burma later in the war he was astonished to bump into another soldier who had been working on sea defences at Dymchurch at the time and the pair realised they had both witnessed the same incident.

Given the date and timing of the crash in the RAF report it was relatively easy to deduce who the pilot might have been. Whilst two Messerschmitt 109s were lost over Britain that day with their pilots unaccounted for only one fitted the time frame for a 17.10 hours loss as quoted by RAF Intelligence. This was the aeroplane flown by the Gruppe Adjutant of Stab II./JG 51, Lt Werner Knittel, who had been flying a Messerschmitt 109 E-4, Werke Nummer 5095, built by the Erla company. Certainly, Knittel was still missing and there were no local burials (even of unidentified airmen) that might be linked to this crash. All the indicators

Lt Werner Knittel, Adjutant of the staff flight of II./JG 51 under the command of Major Werner Mölders, was the pilot of the Me 109 downed at Dymchurch on 28 October 1940. Having failed to return from operations he was posted as missing in action.

pointed to Lt Knittel still being with the wreck of his aircraft.

Thus armed with the official report and local eyewitness information, museum researcher John Elgar-Whinney consulted early post-war aerial photographs taken for the Ordnance Survey and managed to identify the field known as Fielding Land. There on the photograph, and pretty much where the witnesses had indicated, John spotted an almost imperceptible light mark in the field that seemed to indicate either a crater or some other form of unnatural disturbance of the ground.

A site visit was the next step and on 2 June 1973, having secured the landowner's consent, John visited the field to have a look. What he found was promising, and right where the light mark had shown up on the photograph John could see a shallow saucer-like depression of just about fifteen feet or so across. From his knowledge and experience

The excavation of the wreck of Werner Knittel's Me 109 by the Brenzett Aeronautical Museum. This photograph illustrates graphically the difficulties associated with such recoveries and the depth to which crashing aircraft can often penetrate the ground.

it looked very much like a typical aircraft crash impact-crater. A metal detector scan quickly gave readings, and not many inches below the surface he found his evidence in the form of a single fragment of broken aero engine casting that showed signs of violent impact damage. He deduced that this was ground-zero and that the over-revving DB 601 engine had literally torn itself apart on the moment of impact, jettisoning shredded pieces of engine as it had smashed into the ground. Doubtless the impact had also thrown off and fragmented the engine cowling, leaving sufficient shards of yellow-painted alloy on the surface for the crash investigators to find in 1940. John was convinced that the Messerschmitt lay buried deep beneath his feet and a major recovery operation was duly set up for that September.

On Saturday 8 September 1973, the Brenzett team commenced work with a hired mechanical excavator and literally followed downwards a trail of small pieces of aircraft debris that had begun with John Elgar-Whinney's engine fragment. For several more feet there was little else to see, although the soil had clearly been disturbed when compared to the compact marsh clay around what had obviously been the gouge sliced by the crashing aircraft. Here and there on the way down there was the smallest trace of alloy, although the smell of trapped fuel got stronger as the hole got deeper. At a little over thirteen feet the first significant traces of wreckage emerged, and the soil was now visibly stained by oil and petrol. As each bucket load of marsh soil was lifted out it was thoroughly searched by the team. Gradually, more and more pieces of aeroplane emerged until at about eighteen feet the tail oleo leg and wheel were uncovered in what was now a vertical shaft going straight down into the marsh. Using a ladder to access the bottom of the pit, team members could

The force of the terrific impact had literally torn apart the Messerschmitt's DB 601 engine.

see they were now standing on a compressed tangle of wreckage. However, with no shoring and little in the way of safety measures the very act of being in such a deep excavation was hazardous to say the very least; this was unstable ground at the best of times and its integrity had clearly been compromised by the violent impact and burial of several tons of wreckage. Making matters worse, even more tons of machinery were perched at the edge of the excavation with every movement of the digger making the ground shake and tremble like a giant blancmange. Almost twenty feet down in an excavation was not a sensible place to be. Any careful examination and removal of the wreckage by hand was out of the question and the wreckage simply had to be lifted out by the digger, however brutal that might seem. The alternative was that the rest of the wreckage stayed where it was.

By the following day, Sunday 9 September, the excavations had been completed and the team had hauled out an absolute mass of jumbled wreckage from a depth of precisely twenty-five feet and ten inches. It was at this depth that the smashed engine was recorded and the dig finally terminated. Now, it was a case of sifting and sorting what had been pulled out of the ground. At this point, a flying boot was seen sticking out of the wreckage.

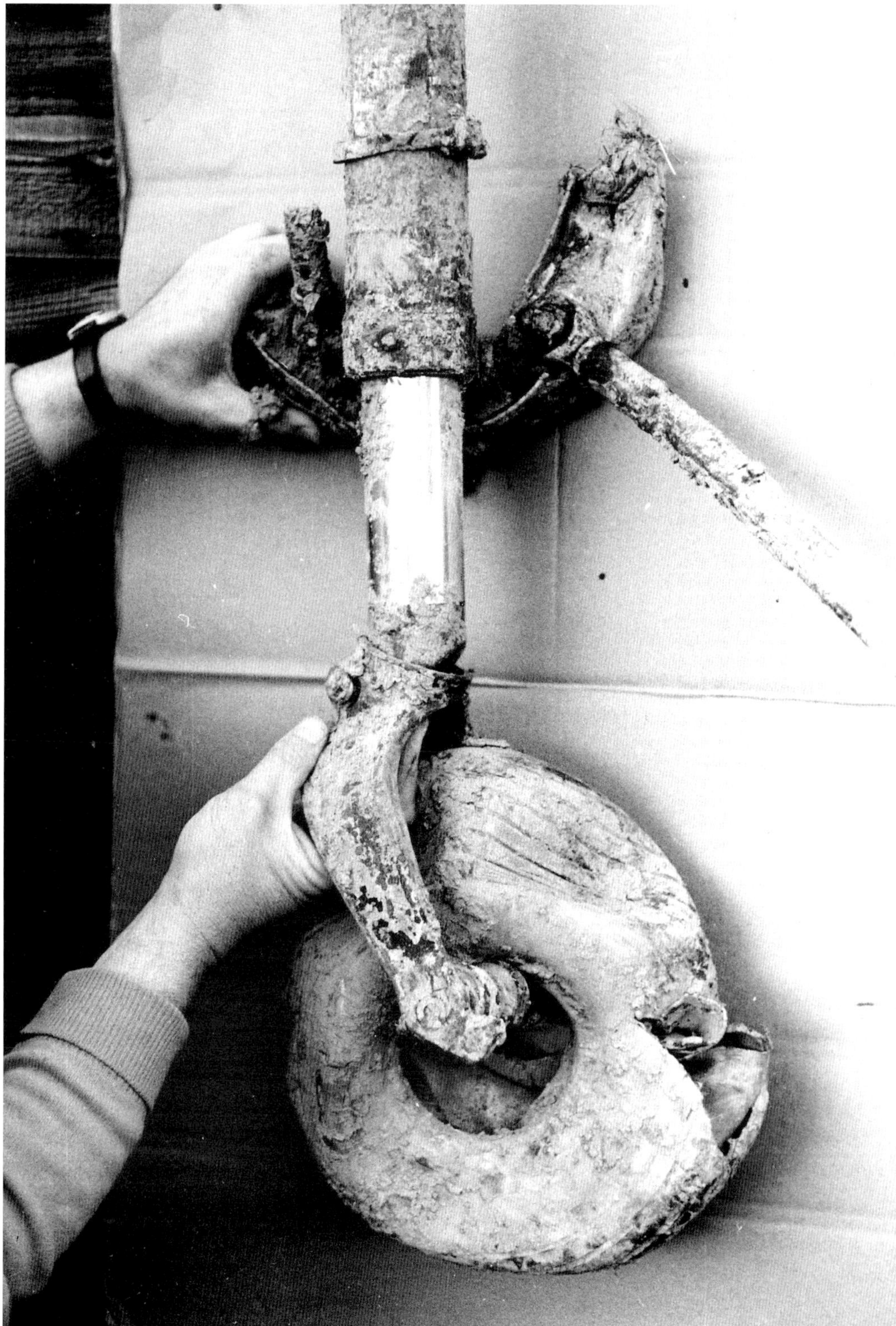

One of the first recognisable finds was the tailwheel of the Messerschmitt 109. Beneath the deeply buried tailwheel the rest of the fuselage was compacted together in a tight mass.

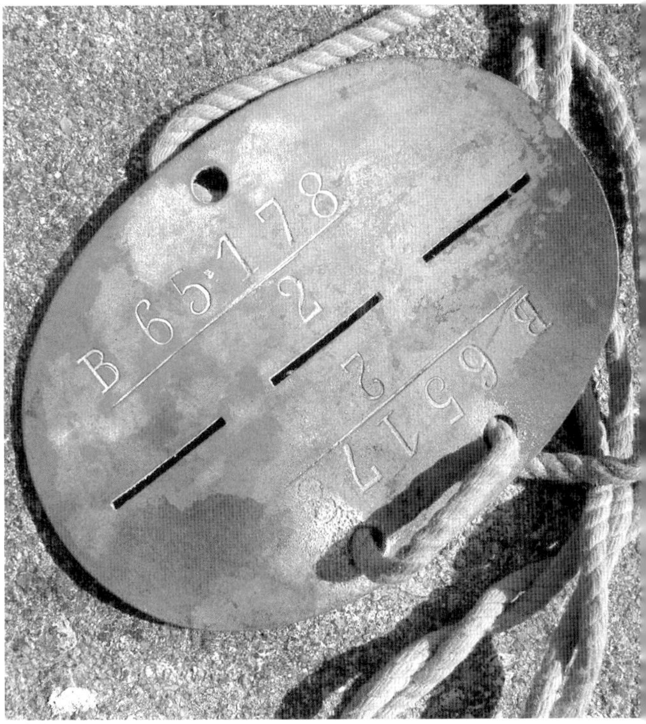

Having been missing since 28 October 1940, Werner Knittel was eventually found during the 1973 excavation by the Brenzett Aeronautical Museum. Proof of his identity was established through the discovery of an identity disc bearing Knittel's service number.

With it there was a packed parachute, lifejacket, scattered personal effects and what would turn out to be a more-or-less complete torso still dressed in a uniform tunic contained within the parachute harness. With the body was an identity disc, bearing the number B 65 178 which, as expected, proved to be an exact match to Werner Knittel. The remains, and the identity disc, were handed into the care of PC John Tomsett of the Kent Police although further examination also revealed a wedding ring which team leader David Buchanan managed to find amongst the wreckage. It was engraved on its inside with the name of the pilot and his bride, Inge. At once, David dispatched it to the West German Embassy in order that it could be returned to the late German officer's wife.

All too often in the past, sensationalist elements of the news media have questioned the motives and activities of those involved with projects of this kind. Generally, they have overlooked or ignored the positive reactions of families when missing casualties are found. In this case, and in specific relation to the wedding ring, David Buchanan quietly and sensitively did the right thing, discreetly and without any fuss, to ensure that it got back to where it belonged; with Inge. Like many similar teams involved in work of this kind the Brenzett group had its detractors in the media of the day, who if the reportage is anything to go by, were not exactly discouraged by the MOD who were clearly feeling embarrassed and awkward about the number of such cases that continued to arise. Indeed, the MOD continued to stick very strongly to the view that these men should neither be recovered nor identified. David Buchanan, and those of his contemporaries who carried out much of this work in the 1970s, surely deserve praise to be heaped upon them and not opprobrium. The saga of Werner Knittel is a case in point.

In what was still an unusual event, HM Coroner Mr John Clark decided that he would need to hold an inquest into the circumstances and identity of the German pilot and his death. However, pre-empting any formal announcement, news of the discovery had appeared in at least three British daily newspapers, *The Sun*, *The Daily Mirror* and *The Daily Mail* on 11 September. On the following day *The Daily Mirror* were again running with the story, this time announcing that the West German Embassy in London were stating that

Although it is not possible to attribute this photograph positively, the image was said by Werner Knittel's widow to show her late husband's aeroplane. Certainly, it depicts a machine of JG 51 and the chevron marking indicates that its pilot was a gruppen adjutant.

Berlin had confirmed the pilot to indeed be Lt Werner Knittel. Opening proceedings at Cranbrook on Tuesday 25 September 1973 Mr Clarke formally identified the pilot by name, albeit two weeks after it had been announced in the news media. After hearing from pathologist Dr Victor Harold Bowers who gave his evidence in relation to the remains, it was established that the cause of death could not be ascertained. All Dr Bowers was able to state was that the body had received multiple fractures consistent with a high velocity impact. After taking all the relevant evidence, including details from David Buchanan as to how the casualty had been located and recovered, Mr Clarke commented that he had previously held the inquest into Plt Off George Drake, the missing RAF Hurricane pilot. In that case, said Clarke, he had issued a death certificate and the family had been very glad to have it. In the case of Werner Knittel he explained that the inquest was being held in order that the widow could obtain a death certificate if she so wished.

Inge Knittel, like many other widows, girlfriends, siblings or parents had at first refused to accept that her man was not coming home. Not long before he was lost he had written: "They'll never get me. I'll outlive the war." Perhaps it was just the common opinion so often spawned in wartime by the need to *believe* in one's own survival. The feeling that convinced combatants that it will always be the other man and it will never be me. Or perhaps, quite understandably, it was Werner's way of reassuring his anxious wife that he was coming home. However, the prospects did not seem good after he failed to return. When Werner had been shot down II Gruppe of JG 51 had been right over the south coast and it seemed very likely that his fighter must have crashed into the English Channel. Hptm Josef Fözö, a Staffelkapitän with II Gruppe, witnessed what happened:

Discovered in the wreckage of the Me 109 was this broken Mont Blanc fountain pen – quite likely the same pen with which Werner Knittel had written home to his wife in order to assure her of his certain survival of the war just prior to going missing in action.

> "I didn't see Knittel's aircraft get hit, but I saw the results. His plane was trailing a long plume of smoke. I saw him drop out of formation and lose altitude fast, diving towards the English coast."

To the pilots of II./JG 51 it was clear that Werner Knittel was not coming home, and although they saw no parachute it was always possible that he had escaped safely although unseen by his colleagues. Another fellow pilot who was sure about Werner's fate was Oblt Günther Matthes, the CO of II/Gruppe JG 51:

> "I remember on that day that with my whole group we were airborne to southern England. Lt Werner Knittel, from Karlsruhe, was my adjutant. He flew right behind me. Maybe ten or twenty metres higher than me, perhaps. He was in my Rotte. Below glittered the thirty-kilometre wide English Channel, like liquid lead in the last rays of sun from the sky. I had ordered 'Free hunting as far as your fuel range!' and the group was beginning to break apart. Instead, it was the English hunters who found us and suddenly they came down on us from a great height with the setting sun at our backs. When I saw the tracer bullets going past I veered away. When I looked back, Knittel was gone. A few minutes later and I had landed at Calais-Mardyck to wait in vain for Knittel but I knew that he wasn't coming back. For me it was clear. My colleague had fallen in the Channel.
>
> "We immediately arranged for our air sea rescue service, already in the area as cover to our mission, to go and search for Werner. Earlier, we had also lost another pilot, Fw John, who had been hit in the oil tank, had baled out but had been seen to fall into the sea with an unopened parachute. Anyway, I waited for two days and then when there was no news I wrote to Werner's wife, Inge. It was a really difficult letter to write because they had only been married just over a year – having got married on 2 September 1939, the eve of war with Britain. Always, he had been an incorrigible optimist and was a huge

This photograph was taken in France shortly before Werner Knittel was killed and shows the commanding officer of II/JG 51, Oblt Günther Matthes, on the left. It fell to Matthes to write to Werner's wife to tell her that her husband was missing. Lt Werner Knittel is standing on the right.

man, in every sense. He was very broad shouldered, and with a wide thin mouth and distinctive features. He was the prototype of a daredevil. Three months earlier the younger of his two brothers had been killed as an infantry man in France, but Werner always said 'Nothing will ever happen to me! We will meet healthy and happy after the war!' and his pretty wife, Inge, wanted to believe those words. Even his parents thought the same. 'Our son is an expert flier. He will have controlled the machine safely', they assured me. But I knew then what the truth was."

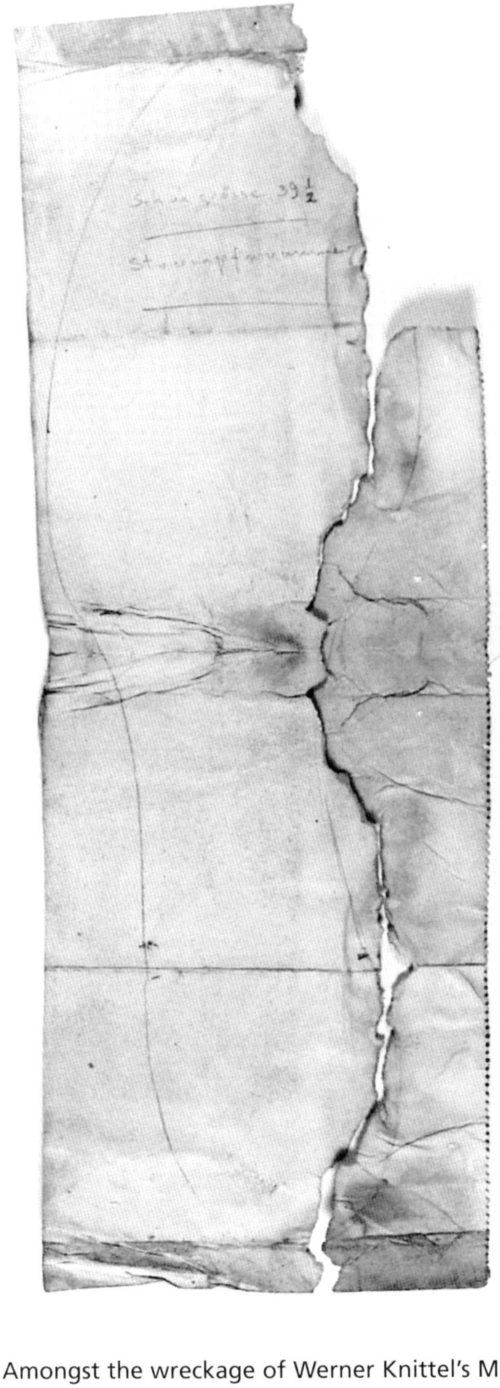

When no news came via the Red Cross after the passage of a few weeks to confirm that he was safe but prisoner of war, things did not look good. And when no news came either that his body had been found his fellow pilots were not surprised and drew their own conclusions; Werner had gone into the English Channel and would never be found. Inge, meanwhile, still clung to hope. After all, had not her husband taken measurements of her feet on his last leave? She had wanted him to get her some shoes in France. The latest Paris fashion, in fact. He had promised her that he would get them, and further promised her that he would always come home safely no matter what. She

Amongst the wreckage of Werner Knittel's Me 109 was discovered a selection of various pieces of paperwork, including this curious pencilled outline of a shoe. In fact, it was his wife's correct shoe size and Werner had intended to take the drawing with him to Paris in order to purchase the latest in fashion footwear for her.

This poignant discovery, eventually returned to Werner Knittel's widow, was his wedding ring engraved on the inside with the names 'Inge' and 'Werner'.

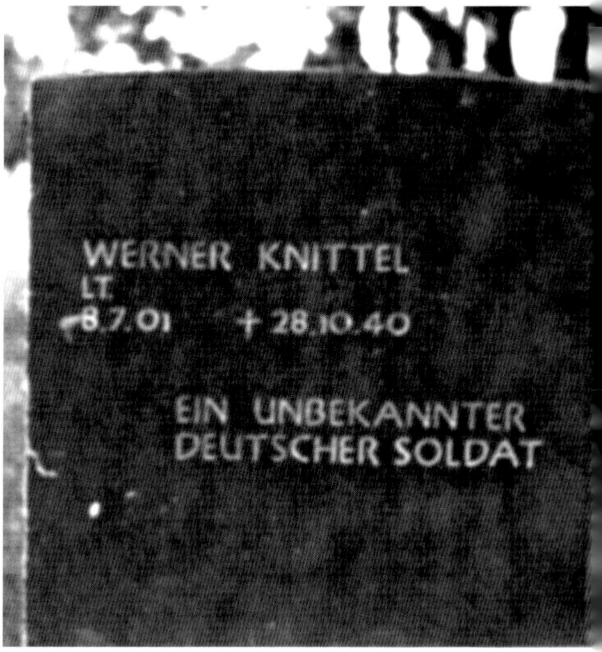

The headstone to Werner Knittel at Cannock Chase German Military Cemetery. The unknown airman buried with him came from the Messerschmitt 110 shot down at Long Bredy, Dorset, on 7 October 1940. (Compare this photograph to that on page 38.)

had to believe him, and continued to do so – whatever common sense eventually dictated. In fact, when in 1942 the German authorities informed her that for official purposes her husband had now been declared dead, she didn't want to believe them either. Throughout the war she clung to that desperate hope of his eventual return and even convinced herself that he would somehow come back when the war was finally over.

Of course, he didn't turn up as she had so desperately hoped and as the years passed the still grieving Inge Knittel could never bring herself to find happiness elsewhere and never re-married. Instead, she threw herself into study and became a doctor of international law. During her studies she also travelled to England, unknowingly passing very close to where her late husband still lay entombed in his Messerschmitt 109. Eventually, Dr Knittel worked at the Paris headquarters of the Western European Union, an international peace-keeping organisation which is where she was employed when news came through of her husband's discovery. Although she attended her husband's military funeral at Cannock Chase German Military Cemetery on 8 October 1973, she remained private in her still evident grief and sadness. However, as she followed her late husband's coffin to its grave site, Inge was at long last able to accept that Werner Knittel was not coming home – thirty-three years after the event. German pastor Jurgen Müller, delivering the eulogy, deplored the horrors of war, going on to say, "We are shocked that so many years after the war we still have to think about it."

Of course, Inge had doubtless thought about it every day since her Werner had vanished and it was, perhaps, somewhat ironic that she should now be working for international peace and still grieving for a man lost during one of the most horrific wars in history. As Inge stood by her husband's graveside, Herr Neumärker, a diplomat from the West German Embassy in London, told her that he had something to give to her and took out of his pocket a small box. Snapping it open, Inge Knittel was staring at Werner's wedding ring. The emotional importance of this small but tangible link to Werner was clearly of the most profound significance. Slipping it into her pocket and biting her lip she must have thought back all those years to 2 September 1939 when she had placed it on his finger.

Intense media interest in the case, some of it garish, appeared in the German newspapers during 1972 and 1973 – even noting that the II Gruppe emblem of JG 51 carried the motto 'Gott strafe England' – or, God Punish England. Naturally, the British news media of the day followed the tale of Werner Knittel's discovery, identification and burial with equally enthusiastic interest. The *Daily Mirror* reported on the story in its 11 September 1973 edition under the headline 'The Last of The Many.' This headline, and the story beneath it, rather inferred that Werner Knittel would be the last of the many missing Luftwaffe casualties from World War Two to be found. In fact, he was to be the *first* of the many.

CHAPTER 2

"To A Gallant Foe"

Gefreiter Richard Riedel, pilot of the Messerschmitt 109 which crashed at Melon Farm, Ivychurch.

BY NOVEMBER 1940 THE Battle of Britain was officially over, although when freshly-trained Messerschmitt 109 fighter pilot Gefr Richard Riedel was posted to 2./JG 3 earlier that month, directly from the Jagdfliegerschule 1 (No 1 Fighter Pilot School) at Merseburg, there was still plenty of action to be had over the island. If Riedel had worried that he would miss the war by the time he got posted to a front-line unit then the Geschwader's regular sorties since his arrival on the Channel coast must have put his mind at rest. An eager young fighter pilot, he was doubtless keen to get into the fray. This is what he had trained for, and all through the spring and summer months of 1940, whilst he had struggled to master the art of flying and fighting with the Me 109, he had eagerly devoured news of the exploits of 'Experten' like Galland, Wick and Mölders in actions over France and then over Britain. He was itching to be there with them.

Richard was still very much a novice pilot, a greenhorn, when he took part in I/JG 3's high-altitude sweep involving about twenty Messerschmitt 109s that ranged out across Kent during the late afternoon of 17 November 1940 and it may well have been his inexperience that ultimately killed him. Unlike most of the other Luftwaffe losses detailed in this volume there is no direct evidence that he fell to RAF guns, although on the other hand we do know that he crashed to his death during an engagement with Spitfires. That day, however, it was icing at high altitude that was an additional enemy for both sides.

By mid afternoon the Spitfires of the Biggin Hill wing (74 and 92 Squadrons) were airborne from around 15.15hrs on a patrol line over Rochford. When they were at 15,000ft the squadrons were informed of enemy activity in the area around Beachy Head and yet more coming in around Brighton. 74 Squadron were vectored westwards towards Brighton, where they ultimately engaged a formation of I./JG 27 Me 109s and managed to shoot one down into the sea, while 92 Squadron had ventured slightly more easterly than their colleagues in an attempt to pick up the force in the Beachy Head area. As they approached Eastbourne at about 16.15 a formation of about twenty aircraft were spotted high above them at around 26,000ft and these were initially taken to be the Spitfires of 74 Squadron.

When they were identified for what they were, Flt Lt J W 'Pancho' Villa led the squadron in and round behind the Me 109s in a climbing turn to attack although, by this time, they were already diving down intending to attack 92 Squadron in a 'bounce'. This was the formation of I./JG 3 Messerschmitts of which group Richard Riedel was part. Chaos inevitably reigned for a few minutes as the two groups of fighters attempted to position themselves for attack, although with the Messerschmitt's speed building up in the dive towards the Spitfires many of the German fighters tore straight through the formation without getting in a shot. Those who did get a bead on a Spitfire were frustrated to find that their guns froze after just a few rounds due to the intense cold at this altitude. Plt Off R H Holland managed to get in a four-second burst on one of the Me 109s from about three hundred yards and saw several puffs of black smoke, but as he closed in to finish it off his windscreen immediately froze over. Three other squadron pilots also claimed inconclusive hits on 109s, whilst Sgt J W Allison was another of 92 Squadron's pilots who registered hits on one of the enemy. He was also unfortunate to be the one RAF pilot in that action who was actually shot at and hit by the Messerschmitts. His combat report tells the story:

> "I was Yellow 2 when we attacked about twenty 109s. I picked out one and fired a couple of short bursts from astern and slightly to one side at 150 yards range. I saw glycol coming from the enemy and a piece of his tail fell off. I had to break away as another 109 was attacking me from behind and I was unable to see if the enemy aircraft had crashed. My 'kite' was badly hit, my engine temperature went off the clock and my machine then caught fire. I selected a field at Kemsing near Sevenoaks to make a forced landing. I followed the prescribed routine, slid back the canopy, opened the door, checked my Sutton Harness was tight and prayed. All did not go well. Spitfire N3229 dug in and stopped abruptly. My face smashed into the gunsight cutting my left eye. After a few seconds I scrambled out and walked away. My ammunition exploded sporadically as my Spitfire burned out."

Of the 92 Squadron pilots who shot at the Me 109s, none were awarded a victory claim. All that could be assessed was that these were damaged or probable victories, although on land RAF Intelligence officers would find the wreck site of one Me 109 at Melon Farm, Ivychurch, in the centre of Kent's Romney Marsh.

As the Me 109s of JG 3 dived down from altitude towards the Spitfires, Gefr Richard Riedel's aircraft was seen to continue in its all-out dive away from the enemy after the German pilots had made their rather abortive attack. In the war diary of I./JG 3 it was noted that he had "no-one on his tail". Of course, it is entirely possible that he was one of the aircraft shot at inconclusively by the Spitfire pilots. After all, it only needed one lucky (or unlucky) hit in the right place to disable a pilot or his machine. On the other hand, and with none of the other JG 3 pilots seeing Riedel hit, there are other causes that might well have resulted in what would turn out to be a terminal dive. The JG 3 war diary noted that perhaps he was seeking refuge in the lower cloud layer and had dived into it so fast that he had no chance to pull out. On the other hand, icing could well have had some catastrophic effect on his flying controls or else he could have simply experienced oxygen failure and blacked out. This was not an uncommon cause of crashes from high altitudes such as those at which the Me 109s were operating that day. Whatever the reason, Richard Riedel's Messerschmitt tore out of the overcast at a terrific speed and, still in a vertical dive, slammed with ground juddering force into the marsh. However, and despite the total destruction that ensued, RAF Intelligence officers were able to report as follows:

> "Me 109. Crashed on 17 November 1940 at 15.30 (sic) at Melon Farm, Ivychurch. Map reference R.4747. Markings not known. Air frame manufactured by Arado F.W. in 1940. Air frame number 1528. Following fighter action aircraft dived into ground at high speed and is almost entirely buried in mud and water. Pilot dead in crater under wreckage. No details regarding armament etc possible."

The excavation of Richard Riedel's aircraft on Kent's Romney Marsh by the Brenzett Aeronautical Museum gets underway during November 1974.

Although it was clear that the unknown pilot was dead and in the wreckage, nothing was done to retrieve his body. In truth, there was nothing then that could have been done. So deep was the

One of the items recovered from the wreck of the Me 109 was this almost straight MG 17 machine gun, still a bright gunmetal blue. Like many items recovered from deeply buried aircraft wrecks the metal remains in pristine condition.

wreckage, and so waterlogged and soft was the ground, that pilot and machine would lie entombed for many more years. Meanwhile, Riedel's family were notified through the usual channels that he was missing presumed killed. Moreover, the aircraft number quoted by RAF Intelligence (1528) was wrong. In fact, Riedel was lost in an Me 109 E-4, Werke Nummer 4898, as research in the 1960s and 70s was to substantiate.

As with the majority of other cases detailed in this book it was, however, inevitable that the crash site would, sooner or later, come under scrutiny by the increasing number of aviation archaeologists working on promising-looking sites in south-east England. That inevitability finally manifested itself during early 1974 when the Brenzett Aeronautical Museum, based just two miles away from the crash site, followed up on reports of the incident and duly located the impact point. Permission to excavate the site was obtained from landowner Brian Frith with the proviso that the team would need to wait until after the harvest that year although the late harvest and prolonged wet weather had hindered plans to set the recovery in motion.

Coincidentally, however, it turned out that Tony Graves and John Tickner of the former London Air Museum were also on the trail of Riedel's Messerschmitt and concurrently turned up on the marsh during October of that year to make their own enquiries. Eventually, the trail led to farmer Brian Frith. Exactly what happened is unclear, but it seems that Mr Frith wrongly assumed the pair to be involved with the Brenzett team who had only recently enquired about the site and he duly gave them authority to excavate there and then since the harvest had now been lifted. Tony and John lost no time in organising a mechanical excavator, and on 30 October 1974 they were on site and set to recover the wreck. A combination of an opportunistic visit by the London Air Museum team and confusion by the landowner as to who was involved looked set to deny the Brenzett team

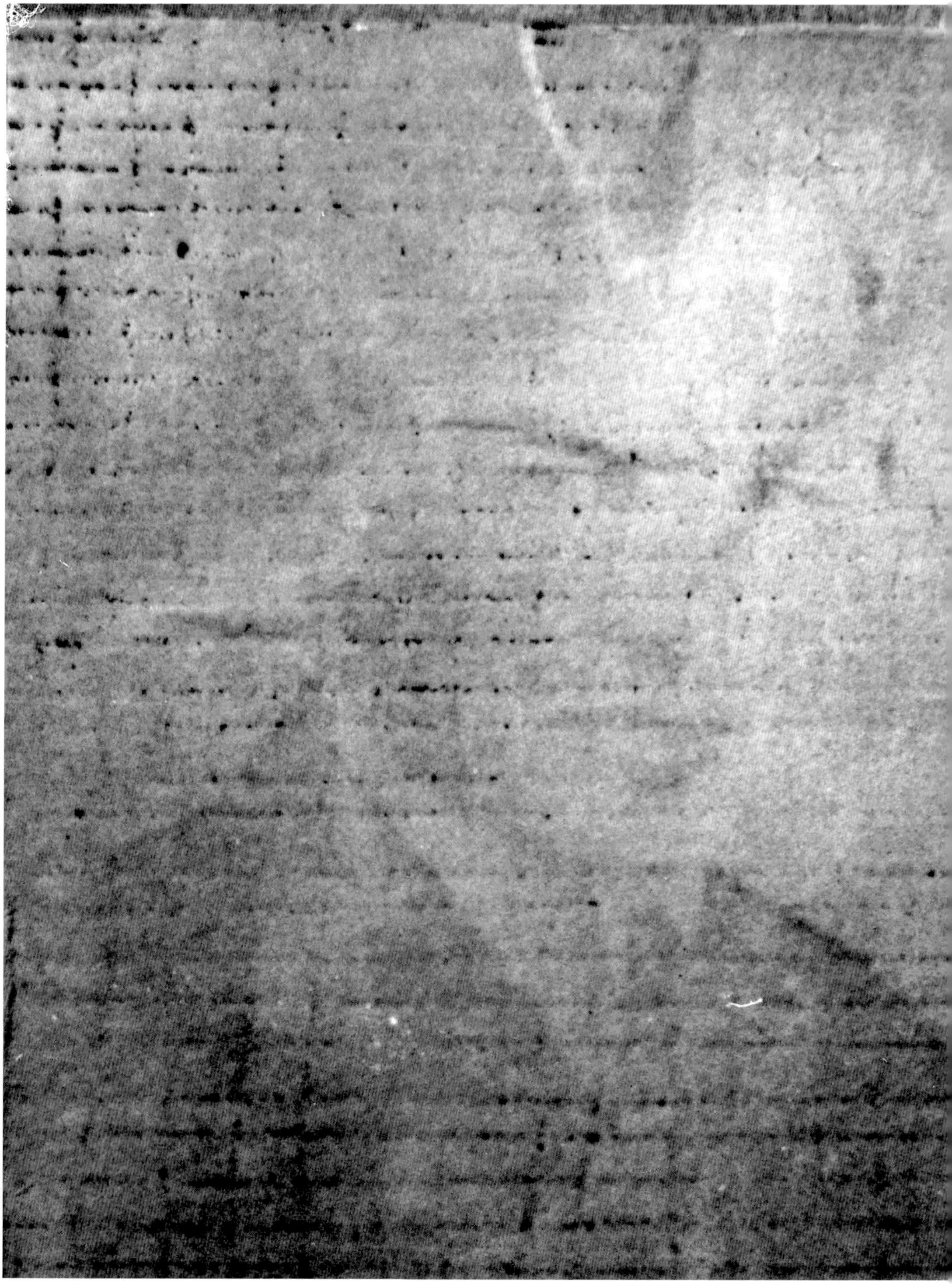

When Riedel's bodily remains were recovered during the Brenzett team's operation a ghostly image of his portrait photograph was found impressed into a wallet lining. Within seconds of this image being exposed to the light, and just a few moments after this photograph had been taken, it simply faded away. Compare this photograph with his portrait picture on page 24.

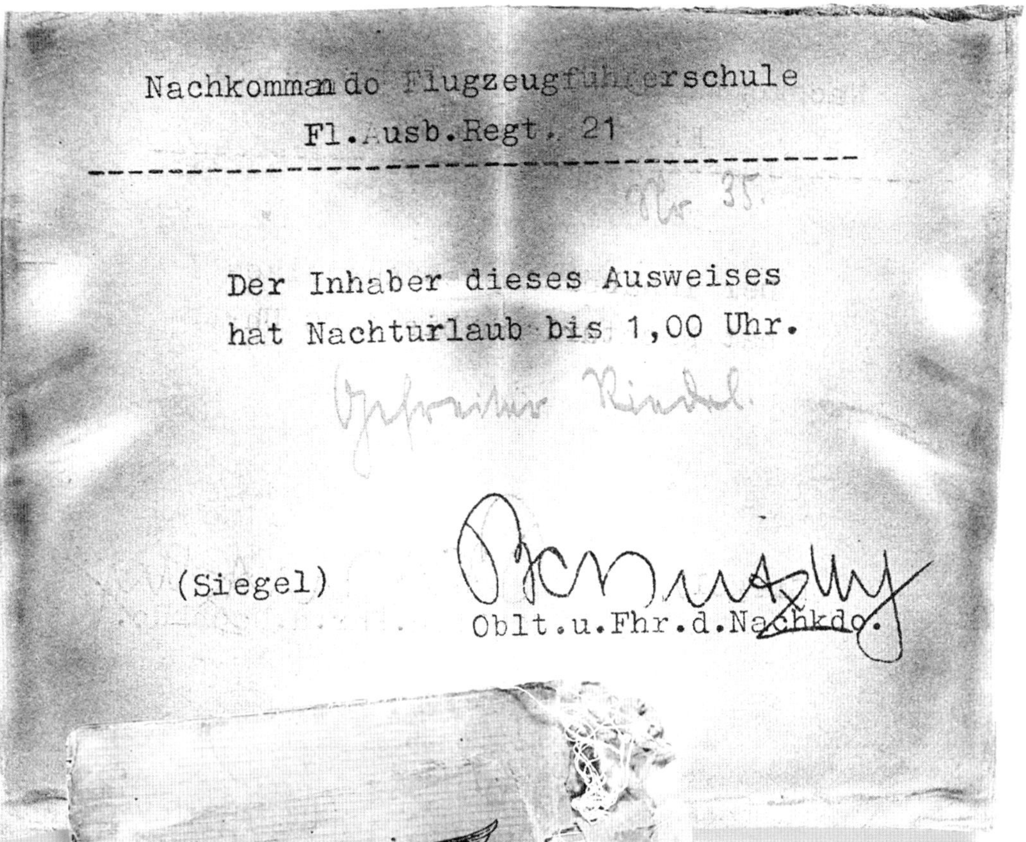

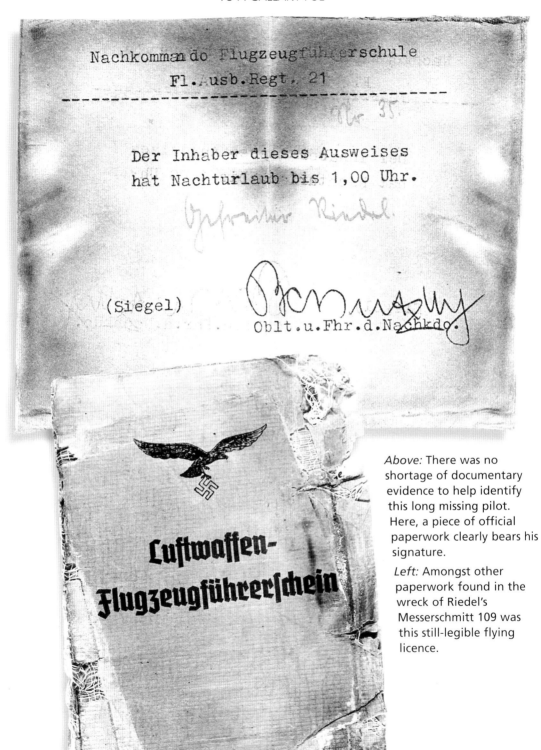

Nachkommando Flugzeugführerschule
Fl.Ausb.Regt. 21

Der Inhaber dieses Ausweises
hat Nachturlaub bis 1,00 Uhr.

(Siegel)

Oblt.u.Fhr.d.Nachkdo.

Above: There was no shortage of documentary evidence to help identify this long missing pilot. Here, a piece of official paperwork clearly bears his signature.

Left: Amongst other paperwork found in the wreck of Riedel's Messerschmitt 109 was this still-legible flying licence.

of the operation they had already set up. However, so deep was the wreckage that the machine hired by the pair ran out of reach and at the extremity of its range the excavator arm fished just the tailwheel assembly and part of the fuselage cross out of the crater. Nothing more. Failing light and an inadequate machine for the task in hand had beaten them.

When the Brenzett team heard of the failed attempt they lost no time in organising what they had planned anyway – a full scale excavation using a long-reach tracked mechanical excavator. The team knew very well the difficulties of digging in the marsh, and when they arrived on site exactly one month later, on 30 November, they had the right kit and knew exactly where to dig. Consequently, and by the end of their operation, they had lifted out the wreckage and had found, too, the remains of its pilot. Although the formalities of identification through the local coroner had yet to be concluded the team knew almost at once that this was Richard Riedel when a large quantity of his personal paperwork came to light, all of it clearly named to him. Not only that but his identity disc, still looped onto its string necklace, and also a piece of metal with the number of the aircraft, 4898, were found jumbled in the wreckage. Included in that wreckage was Richard Riedel's flying licence bearing a faded and ghostly image of the long lost flier. Eerily, the photograph faded before the eyes of the recovery team when it emerged into the light, although not before its vanishing image was photographed for the record.

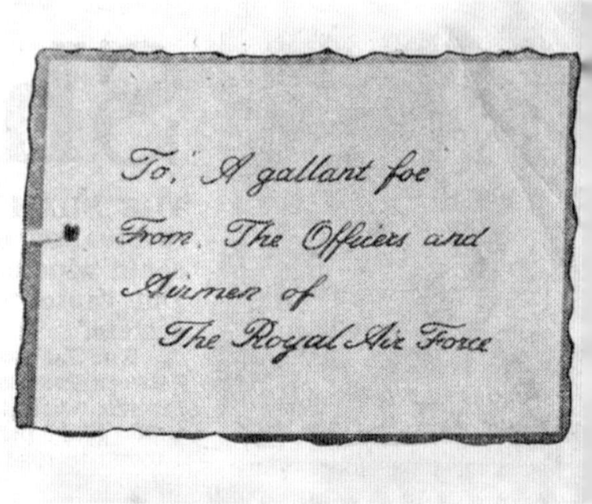
To, A gallant foe
From, The Officers and
Airmen of
The Royal Air Force

When Richard Riedel was finally laid to rest in the German Military Cemetery at Cannock Chase his funeral was conducted by his former enemy, the Royal Air Force. This moving tribute was attached to a wreath from the officers and men of the RAF.

By 2 December that year the West German Embassy in London had confirmed the identity of Richard Riedel and this was being widely announced in the British mainstream daily newspapers, albeit that *The Sun* were somewhat inaccurately describing Riedel as an ace fighter pilot under a headline: 'Dead War Ace Found in Marsh'. A case of never letting the facts get in the way of a good story, perhaps. Despite the fact that the formalities of naming the pilot had been somewhat pre-empted by the news media it fell again to East Kent Coroner Mr John Clarke to call a formal inquest at Ashford, Kent, on 9 December 1974 in what were now becoming increasingly common proceedings for him. Once more he stated that the inquest was being called in order officially to name the man and to issue a death certificate for Richard Riedel if his next of kin wished for one. At the end of the hearing, the identity of the body had been established in British law and Riedel was no longer on the missing list.

In what was a remarkably rapid conclusion to events following his discovery during November, Richard was buried with full military honours at Cannock Chase German Military Cemetery on 19 December 1974. Very often in cases like these, and as we shall see in others in this book, the period between discovery and formal interment can be a very long one indeed. In this case the funeral was held less than three weeks after he was found. Sadly, his relatives were living in what was then communist East Germany and were obviously unable to attend although it is understood that they had been formally notified via the International Red Cross of the discovery. If there were no floral tributes from the Riedel family, constrained as they were behind the Iron Curtain, there was an impressive wreath from the RAF. On its card was a simple message: "To a gallant foe. From the officers and airmen of The Royal Air Force."

CHAPTER 3 Incident at Long Bredy

FOLLOWING HOT ON THE heels of the discovery in Kent of Werner Knittel amongst the wreckage of his Messerschmitt 109 (See Chapter One) other enthusiasts much further west had also located and started to excavate another Messerschmitt lost during October 1940 – this time a Messerschmitt 110 shot down on the 7th of that month at Kingston Russell Dairy Farm in the little Dorset village of Long Bredy. Here, at quarter past four in the afternoon, the headmaster of nearby Litton Cheney Primary School had stepped outside with his binoculars to watch an air battle taking place high above him. Through his binoculars John Bailey saw the aircraft singled out for attention by British fighters at around 15,000ft, heard the rat-tat-tat of machine-gun fire, and then saw the Me 110 on which he had focussed roll over onto its back. Streaming black smoke from both engines the German plane nosed forward until, quite vertical, it entered what would become a terminal earth-bound plummet. Both engines roared at full throttle, but still pouring black smoke and sparks.

Initially, Bailey thought he'd see the plane pull out of its dive. Although it was clearly in trouble, maybe the pilot was just trying to get away from his attackers? Or maybe the pilot was trying to extinguish the burning motors? As he watched it on its vertical path, Bailey realised that neither was the case. Instead, he waited for the white blossom of two parachutes as the crew abandoned the aircraft but the plane just continued its downward path. It neither turned nor deviated from its arrow-like trajectory, and as it got closer he could clearly see sunlight glinting off the canopy Perspex and the German crosses on its wings.

Travelling at perhaps around four hundred miles per hour the Messerschmitt finally flashed out of sight, still vertical, beyond the tree line and the hills. The awful din of the over-revving Daimler-Benz engines was snuffed out momentarily after the aircraft had been lost to view and just before a dull thud reverberated across the Dorset pastures towards him. From where it had vanished, the faintest wisp of black smoke drifted lazily upwards and then was gone. Overhead, the sounds of a retreating air battle came back into auditory range, having been completely drowned out by the diving fighter. Away to the south now were the signs of rapidly departing German aircraft. An occasional and almost desultory rattle of gunfire could also be heard against the sound of numerous returning RAF fighters heading back northwards.

A matter of just a minute or two had elapsed from when the first signs of an air battle overhead had developed to when the Messerschmitt had dived out of the heavens and to when the sky was all but clear of aeroplanes again. Such was the brevity of an aerial combat. Those who witnessed them, like John Bailey for instance, forever held vivid memories of those engagements as if they were frozen in a moment of time or else they were replayed over and over again, almost film-like, in their mind's eye.

On the ground at Long Bredy those venturing into the field called Brickhills found a patch of disturbed soil on the slope leading down from a little copse and just two hundred yards east north east from the dairy buildings. It looked almost as if some giant agricultural rotovator had churned up a small plot in the middle of the grazing meadow. Tiny shreds of aluminium glinted silver in the late afternoon weak autumn sun. Otherwise, there was nothing to show that an aeroplane had fallen here. The stench of petrol hung heavy on the air, and strange creaking and groaning noises emerged from the cracked clods of clay. Beneath ground the wreckage was sinking and cooling and the earth that had cascaded on top of it gradually collapsed back into the violently hewn crater. It was hard for those arriving to have a look to comprehend exactly how the aeroplane had so completely vanished and left no trace. Equally, it is sometimes difficult for those reading of such events to appreciate how an aircraft like this could completely bury itself.

However, one has to consider that this sleekly streamlined aircraft had struck soft ground from an altitude of at least 15,000ft – possibly even more. Each engine with its ancillaries weighed in at nigh on a ton, and the airframe itself weighed a good few tons more. In total, the overall flying weight of the Me 110 was reckoned to be just shy of 7,000kg. Quite likely it had also been touching four hundred mph when it struck, and the impact had been like slicing a hot knife into butter. There was certainly very little for those who had come to gape to actually see. All they could do was marvel at the spectacle that had caused the ground to swallow it up, and to speculate as to what had become of the crew. The RAF intelligence officer who came to report on the crash could only guess, too.

In his assessment, the un-named officer from the RAF's Air Intelligence AI(g) department noted in Report No 3/99 :

> "Me 110. Crashed on 7.10.40 at 16.15 hours at Kingston Russell House, Long Bredy. Map reference U.0010. Following fighter action aircraft dived vertically from a great height with smoke coming from both engines. Engines completely buried and little left of aircraft. Crew two; one believed to have baled out and the other dead in crash. One small nameplate showed the name MIAG. Owing to condition of crash no further details possible."

Clearly, nothing of any useful intelligence value was ever going to be obtained from this wreck. Whatever was there was buried way out of reach. No useful purpose would have been served by digging down to the wreckage even assuming anyone could reach it. As for 'the missing crewman' believed to be in the aircraft there would be no attempt to find him and the crash site was swiftly forgotten by the authorities. It was just one of scores exactly like it and very little effort was ever made in cases of this kind to make anything other than a token or cursory effort to look for crew members – even if any effort was ever made at all! Thus it was that the Long Bredy Messerschmitt crash site remained all but forgotten until 1972. Although villagers still talked about it, the discussions had often centred around the fate of the crew; did they bale out or had they died in the crash?

Some still took the view that the crew had parachuted out a long way away. Certainly, the RAF intelligence officer in 1940 had been led to believe that at least one had baled out. Others, like headmaster John Bailey, were certain. Nobody had escaped from this aircraft before it crashed. It was a certainty shared, apparently, by the parish vicar Canon Frotman who is said to have performed a memorial service in Long Bredy church, complete with honour guard and firing party – but with no bodies to bury. Local legend also had it that some bodily remains had been found in the crash crater but due to parish hostility they had simply been re-buried at the crash site, allegedly thus leading to Canon Frotman's symbolic service. The same legend also has it that locals knew there were two crew members because (sic) "two pairs of flying boots were found". It is said that because of this grim find two white crosses were placed in the adjacent hedge, each marked with the inscription "A German Soldier".

If the white cross story is correct then all trace of the markers had vanished by the 1970s along with any credible recollection of their existence. It is also somewhat strange, surely, that no mention is made of any discovery of the bodily remains of two crew members in the contemporary RAF intelligence report which one would expect to have led to confirmation that both crew were dead. As to the tale about two pairs of flying boots, later discoveries at the site would prove this legend to be just that. So, and whilst a certain degree of local hearsay and folklore had grown up around the incident across the years, the challenge during the 1970s was to extract the fact from the fiction. It was also to find out who the two crew members involved were.

On 7 October 1940 the Luftwaffe had launched a significant attack against the Westland aircraft factory at Yeovil, with twenty-five Junkers 88s of II/KG 51 detailed for the raid which took place during the late afternoon and with close-escort being provided by fifty Messerschmitt 110s of II and III Gruppen of ZG 26. To an extent these aircraft were well suited to the task of long-range escort since the distances involved in the flight crossed the widest part of the English Channel between the Cherbourg peninsula and Dorset. On the other hand, when it came to close-combat (dog-fighting) with the more manoeuvrable Spitfires and Hurricanes they were not always best suited or well matched in battle against the RAF fighters. However, the range involved that day, which also included an inland leg of some twenty-odd miles from the English coast, meant that the otherwise more suited escort fighters, the Messerschmitt 109s, simply did not have the range. Instead, some thirty Me 109s had taken the bombers just to the English coast and then had to turn for home.

Critical fuel levels had meant that the Ju 88s and the heavy Me 110 escorts were on their own. Alerted to the incoming raid by the RDF radar stations RAF Fighter Command were waiting; 56, 152, 238, 601 and 609 Squadrons were up and ready with their massed formations of Spitfires and Hurricanes long before the enemy formations had neared the south coast. With ample warning the squadrons also had the advantage of height, with 609 Squadron's Spitfires already at 20,000ft and visibility exceptional. From this altitude the pilots airborne over Dorset could see Swansea and the south coast of Wales. Away to the south could be seen France and the Channel Islands whilst eastwards, beyond the Isle of Wight, the tip of Selsey Bill was visible. Conditions were perfect for the RAF's interception – including good weather and tactical advantage. As the German formation crossed the coast around Weymouth the RAF fighters tore into them.

As with many aerial combats it is often difficult to sort out exactly which pilot shot down which aircraft and the battles over Dorset on the late afternoon of 7 October 1940 are no exception. In respect of the Long Bredy Messerschmitt, however, it seems most likely that the victor must have been the 609 Squadron CO, Sqn Ldr Michael Robinson in Spitfire L1096, PR-L. Ten miles north west of Portland, and with 238 Squadron's Hurricanes flying off to 609's left, Robinson closed in on one of the Me 110s after it had been shot at by a Hurricane. He attacked from dead astern and saw it dive vertically into the ground about five miles north of the coast. The timing, geography and description is pretty much a near-perfect match.

During the combat over Dorset's coastal hills more than just the single Me 110 at Long Bredy had been shot down with no less than seven aircraft from various elements of ZG 26 falling to British fighters. Of these losses, though, only two crews were classified as missing; Ofw Fritz Stahl with Uffz Ernst Mauer of 4./ZG 26 and Ofw Karl Herzog and Obegefr Herbert Schilling of 6./ZG 26. Of the other losses, some had involved casualties and others were POWs. Some had been shot down into the sea, and of these at least one crew had baled out – Oblt H Grisslich and Uffz L Obermeir taking to their parachutes with Grisslich landing in the sea and Obermeir coming down on land. Given that this was at the same time as the Long Bredy crash, and Obermeir's descent was only a few miles distant from there, it is very likely that he was the man RAF intelligence had initially and incorrectly linked to the Long Bredy crash. However, when enthusiasts started to look at the site in 1972 there were only two missing crews who could be considered; Stahl and Mauer or Herzog and Schilling. No real clues existed to indicate which crew it might be.

To local enthusiasts Barry Northam, Peter Nash and Michael Dodge the Messerschmitt crash at Long Bredy was a curious mystery that begged further investigation. Inspired by the notion that tangible relics of the Me 110 might be extant at the crash site, the trio set out to look for it by following local leads and clues. Eventually, and after a long search, they pinned down the impact point during 1972 and set about excavating the site after obtaining the landowner's consent. At a depth of sixteen feet the team found aircraft wreckage, personal effects and human remains during a dig on 13 October 1973 and in view of their discoveries they suspended operations and handed over their finds to the care of HM Coroner for Central Dorset, Mr Morris Bailey. Amongst the discoveries were uniform material, a wallet, handkerchief, a gold-plated cross, unopened parachute and charred books and notebooks.

Of these items the handkerchief gave the most promise for providing evidence of identification since it had the initials RB embroidered in one corner. Unfortunately, though, it didn't help. There were simply no missing crew members from that day who had those initials and this was seemingly a red-herring. However, had they looked further in the wreckage recovered they would almost certainly have found a clue amongst the airframe remains in the form of the airframe Werke Nummer. That alone would have been sufficient to put a name to the crew. Ultimately, there was nothing then found or identified by which to name the remains and they were duly buried at Cannock Chase German Military Cemetery as unknown. Of course, that wasn't the end of the story.

Another local historian, the inveterate aviation archaeologist Peter Foote, had long been interested in the site (he had been researching wartime aircraft incidents literally since the war and had been interviewing witnesses since at least the 1950s) and in 1976 he suggested to the Wealden Aviation Archaeological Group that they might like to make some further excavations at the site since it was clear that the 1972 operations there had failed to recover properly all that remained. Indeed, another of the early aviation archaeologists, Al Brown, had also visited the crash site not long after the 1972 dig and discovered a complete set of Luftwaffe air maps, still legible and in a tight bundle, laying on the surface of the field and left behind by the earlier excavators.

Therefore, and following on from Al's visit and Peter Foote's encouragement it was in the August of 1976 that the WAAG team carried out a further dig by mechanical excavator and

Amongst items of wreckage recovered during the 1976 excavation was a damaged signal flare pistol.

recovered considerable quantities of the buried wreckage, retrieved from depths down to almost twenty-five feet. Some of the first finds included scraps left behind or that had been re-buried during 1972 and noteworthy amongst these previously discarded pieces was a small data plate bearing the stamped number 3418. Also significant amongst the more deeply buried wreckage, however, were further personal effects and aircrew remains and whilst the efforts in 1972 had defied identification the discovery of the number 3418 tied this incident to the crew of Karl Herzog and Herbert Schilling. Just to confirm that this crew could certainly be linked to the aeroplane number, however, a recovered diary was marked as the property of Schilling and in a wallet were two cardboard locker tags, one marked Herzog and the other marked Schilling. Almost thirty-six years after the event at least one Luftwaffe crew were no longer missing.

As the wreckage was sifted and examined, so a pair of Luftwaffe flying boots once worn by Herbert Schilling came to light, trapped within the wreckage that had once been his rear cockpit. Inside the boots were three fired 7.92mm cartridge cases – exactly where they had tumbled during the brief engagement as Schilling had desperately blazed away at his attackers with his MG 15 machine gun. The remains of another boot came to light close to a cloth Luftwaffe pilot's badge, both obviously the property of the pilot Karl Herzog, and pieces of another boot were found amongst other wreckage. In themselves they were not hugely significant finds, although they put to rest the legend of two pairs of flying boots having been found there in 1940. Since the boots were buried at over twenty feet inside the wrecked cockpit there is no possibility that they could have been thrown back or re-buried at the time of the crash. With identification now absolute it seemed clear that the remains buried at Cannock Chase could now be named and no doubt the further finds of remains buried with them. Unfortunately, it wasn't that simple.

After the two men had been formally identified by the German authorities they were interred at Cannock Chase with Werner Knittel, the first missing Luftwaffe airman to be found in Britain post-war. Compare this image with that on page 22 depicting the same headstone.

Coroner Morris Bailey, a World War Two naval veteran, had conducted his enquiries in relation to the earlier 1972 finds and had then directed that pathologist Dr Blades examine the skeletal remnants. Despite extensive enquiries arising from the few clues available in both the personal effects and mortal remains, nothing could be found to tie down who these men were and it was this failure to identify that would ultimately lead to their burial at Cannock Chase as

This array of personal effects, including a partial uniform, was found with the body of Herbert Schilling at Long Bredy, Dorset, when the wreckage of his Messerschmitt 110 was unearthed during 1976. Shot down and missing since 7 October 1940, these items helped to identify the two crew members. Of particular significance were the two locker name tags made out to Ogefr Schilling and his comrade, Ofw Karl Herzog.

On 7 October 1940, the same day that the Messerschmitt 110 had been shot down at Long Bredy, this Messerschmitt 109 was one of many other Luftwaffe losses that day. Shot down much further east, and just off the Kent coast at Dymchurch, the pilot of this aircraft (Lt Meyer) had survived to become a prisoner of war. However, the images here are both illustrative and representative of the very many German aircraft downed in the seas around Britain. Of these, hundreds of aircrew were never found although many were later washed ashore but not identified. Some aircraft like this doubtless still lie in deep water with their crews, although any prospects of the recovery or identification of those men is certainly slim.

unknowns. As it happened, they would end up being buried in the same grave as Werner Knittel (see Chapter One). Now, with Coroner Bailey being presented with yet further remains and clear identification it seemed inevitable that an inquest would be re-opened, the men duly named, relatives informed and appropriate named burials at Cannock Chase bringing an end to the story. By now, readers will not be surprised to learn that this was not how things turned out.

On Battle of Britain Day, Wednesday 15 September 1976, the *Dorset Evening Echo* announced that the coroner had no intention of re-opening any enquiries despite the further finds of human remains and freshly discovered clear evidence that pointed with absolute certainty to the men's identities. Instead, Morris Bailey ordered the destruction of the second find of remains and, when asked about his decision, merely stated brusquely: "A lot of people spent a lot of time and trouble earlier on this matter." As far as he was concerned there was no merit in re-opening or re-examining the case. It was a matter of case closed. It was also an astonishing decision, although readers of *Finding The Few* will know that this was not the first time a coroner in such a case had made what many might consider to be a questionable ruling.

Understandably, the Wealden group were dismayed at this turn of events after so much effort had gone into finding and identifying the two fliers. Now, and if HM Coroner's diktat was to be followed through, there would be no hope of Karl Herzog and Herbert Schilling having a marked grave. Not only that, but the second find of remains (primarily those of Herbert Schilling) would be arbitrarily and judicially destroyed. Worse, two families in Germany would now have no hope of ever finding out what happened to their kin. Since this was not a scenario acceptable to the WAAG they immediately made direct contact with the Deutsche Kriegsgräberfürsorge (German War Graves Service) with news of the discovery and informing them as to the evidence of identification.

It was not long before matters moved effectively to overturn the coroner's earlier ruling and order, although acting independently of the coroner the German war graves authority had decided unilaterally that the remains already at Cannock Chase, and the ones more recently discovered, were indeed those of Herzog and Schilling. Pre-empting the destruction of the second set of remains the German authorities requested these be turned over to them for burial, and in an utterly bizarre and surreal twist the superintendent of the Cannock Chase cemetery received notification that he would shortly be receiving the 'new' remains for burial – by postal delivery! In due course, and in an act that can only be viewed as exceedingly disrespectful, the remains were delivered to Cannock Chase via Royal Mail.

With Karl Herzog and Herbert Schilling now afforded a marked grave, and with both men removed from the list of the missing, the Wealden Aviation Archaeological Group could rest on their laurels. Almost. All that now remained was to find the respective relatives or next of kin in Germany but with the Herzog family apparently in what was then communist East Germany the trail in the hunt for them went cold. Eventually, however, after a long search the son of Herbert Schilling was traced to Hamburg by the author. Hans Schilling, writing in 1986, said that whilst his family had been shocked to be told the news in 1977 it had given them some peace at last. Hans went on to say how pleased he was to hear from England about the discovery and went on to ask for photographs of the crash site at Long Bredy and of his father's grave. Had it not been for the efforts of those involved with the 1976 recovery, and their determination to countermand the coroner's decision, then both Herbert and his comrade in arms would still be missing.

CHAPTER 4

"A Service was Held at The Site..."

THE RAPIDITY OF GERMAN air activity directed against the British Isles by the Luftwaffe during the summer months of 1940 had shown no sign of abating as August drifted on into September. Indeed, on 2 September that tempo had perceptibly increased with the Luftwaffe launching no less than almost one thousand sorties – primarily against the south of England. The operations which form the backdrop to the incident with which this chapter is concerned were the attacks directed that day against Eastchurch and Detling aerodromes.

Shortly before noon the Germans were detected by RDF radar stations beginning to mass over the Straits of Dover and by 12.15 the assembly of forces had been completed as the formations swung towards the English coast. By 12.20 a group of between thirty and fifty aircraft came in at Hythe and flew in the general direction of Chatham via Ashford. Ten minutes later another three forces totalling over one hundred aircraft advanced on Dover and, crossing the coast, also converged towards Chatham whilst at the same time some forty aircraft came into the Thames estuary via North Foreland. Watching the developing raids on their plotting boards, RAF controllers were doubtless struggling to second-guess the intended target or targets although the course might have at first suggested the naval installations at Chatham were most likely the objective. However, since airfields had regularly been the main Luftwaffe targets since mid-August then the possibility of RAF Fighter Command sector stations north of the estuary being on the 'hit list' could not be ignored. This seemed especially likely since the force that had come in near North Foreland had headed for the Essex coast.

Whatever the target, Fighter Command needed effectively to counter the threat and no less than eleven squadrons were scrambled between 12.05 and 12.30 with six of these being sent to patrol north of the Thames and the rest being sent down to intercept in the area of Maidstone, Chatham and Rochford just before another six RAF squadrons were ordered off with two orbiting their bases and the other two (43 and 501) vectored towards Maidstone. With nearly four hundred aircraft in the air over Kent and the Thames estuary, the sight and sound to those watching from down below during that Monday lunchtime must have been awesome. The more so when battle was finally joined.

Shortly after 12.45 the Spitfires of 603 Squadron, flying at around 22,000ft, spotted the enemy somewhere around the Isle of Sheppey as anti-aircraft fire exploded around a formation of some forty or fifty Dornier 17s flying below their Spitfires at 15,000ft and trailing an escort of attendant Me 109s. Other 109s, too, were seen 1,000ft above 603 Squadron obviously flying as top cover to the bomber formation, ready and waiting to 'bounce' any would-be attackers of the Dornier force from high out of the sun. Sqn Ldr George Denholm, leading 603 Squadron somewhere about five miles east of Sheppey, put his Spitfires in line-astern, climbing to attack those above and to cut off or impede their expected assault. Diving down on the tempting formations below would, at least initially, have placed 603 Squadron at a tactical disadvantage and surely have invited the higher force of 109s to descend on them like a ton of bricks. Given that the Me 109s above comprised ten vics of about eight or nine aircraft each then the immediate odds were stacked against the squadron, anyhow. Plt Off Morton, in Spitfire N3056, was one of those who climbed to intercept. He described his engagement with the 109s in his combat report:

> "They circled to attack us from astern and we turned also. I met one Me 109 head-on and gave a short burst with no effect. After a while the general melee became split up. I found one Me 109 unattended climbing above me and gave chase. Opened fire from 300 yards on port quarter and slightly below at 23,000ft. Enemy aircraft saw me and did a steep left hand turn into a dive. I got in a good long burst and observed much white smoke from below the enemy aircraft. The aircraft then went into a vertical dive and I did not see it again.
>
> "Plt Off Berry who was in the vicinity reports having seen the aircraft dive vertically into the ground. Enemy aircraft was grey with very light wing tips."

Given the timing and location of the combat, and confirmation by Plt Off Berry that he had seen Morton's victim dive into the ground, identifying the wreck site is quite simple.

Only the evening beforehand, this same patch of sky had also been the battleground of 603 Squadron's Spitfires when Sgt Jack Stokoe had literally chased an Me 109 into the ground at Hurst Farm, Chilham, causing the enemy machine to cartwheel and burst into flames killing its pilot Oblt Otto Bauer of III./JG 53 as the aeroplane tore itself apart across Bush Field. The hapless soldiers who had guarded the wreck, and who were still there the following lunch-time, must have been riveted to the spot when the howl of another Messerschmitt 109 came towards them vertically and at full throttle. At first, it seemed as if it would smash into the ground at the very same spot but the plummeting fighter, trailing a banner of white smoke, veered off and eventually smashed into the ground a little over two hundred yards from where they stood. This, the second Me 109, had crashed into a beet field on Mr Colthup's farm at Mountain Street just to the south west of Chilham leaving precious little for investigators to find as the briefest of RAF intelligence reports clearly indicates:

> "Me 109 crashed two hundred and fifty yards away from the previously reported machine at Chilham, Kent, on 2 September 1940 at 12.55 hours following fighter action. Aircraft lies buried in the ground and is a complete wreck. No identification markings visible."

Unlike the aeroplanes flown by Werner Knittel and Richard Riedel detailed in the previous chapters, this Me 109 had not plunged into soft marsh land to be swallowed up by the peaty clay. The field at Chilham was quite hard loamy soil, interspersed with outcrops of flint and with the chalk of the North Downs beneath. And yet the Messerschmitt had still been driven deep underground by the impact. On the fate of the pilot, the RAF report was silent. Despite this, local knowledge was quite clear that he had not escaped. Indeed, the chief clerk of East Ashford Rural District Council was able to write: "The remains of the pilot are still buried under the engine".

Oblt Ekkehard Schelcher, pilot of the Messerschmitt 109 shot down at Chilham.

Given the timing and location of Morton's claim, and the lack of any other losses of Messerschmitt 109s that could be tied to it, there seems to be very little doubt that this was the aircraft shot down by the 603 Squadron pilot.

Despite the fact that the chief clerk to the local council was aware that the pilot's remains were buried with his aircraft, no attempt was made to recover him. Subsequently, it has become clear that his identity was known to the British authorities. Writing in 1974 the Commonwealth War Graves Commission confirmed that they were aware of this site and its status as a quasi-war grave. They were able to report that the pilot was Oblt Ekkehard Schelcher Stab III./JG 54 and comment on the details recorded within their files:

> "As the machine was still loaded with cannon shells and other explosive material the military, air force and regional health officers decided that both machine and body should be left where they were. A service was held with full military honours and the site was covered over."

By July 1975 the site had come under scrutiny by researcher the late Al Brown who had sought permission from the landowner to excavate it. Mindful of knowledge that some kind of formal funeral service had taken place there, and that the spot had once been marked by a cross, farmer Colthup was disinclined to allow any interference with the site at all. All the same, Al Brown was not to be deterred. Given that the cross had long since vanished, and that technically a missing pilot was clearly involved, Al wrote to the coroner for the Canterbury and Dover district of Kent to see if something could be done officially. With Chilham just two or three miles distant from Canterbury he naturally concluded that Mountain Street fell within the jurisdiction of the coroner based in Canterbury, Mr Wilfred

The recovery of Oblt Schelcher's aircraft at Chilham, Kent, carried out by the Territorial Army, underway during October 1977.

R Mowll, to whom he had enquired about having the wreck officially recovered. Writing back, Mr Mowll explained that in fact the site was outside his district and fell under the responsibility of the coroner for Ashford and Shepway although he had, nonetheless, sent his coroner's officer, PC Tudor, to make initial investigations. Reporting back, Tudor explained that Mr Colthup was reluctant to give any permission for an excavation. Since a coroner had no power to order any such excavation in cases like this the matter would have to be left to rest.

However, the crash site was fairly well known amongst those involved with aviation archaeology in the 1970s and Mr Colthup must have had quite a regular procession of visitors beating a track to his door asking about it, not least of all Tony Graves of the London Air Museum who also sought the backing of the Schelcher family for a recovery. Meanwhile, the Kent Battle of Britain Museum had not long moved into its new premises at Chilham Castle, the stately home of Lord Maserene and Ferrand, which literally overlooked the site. Clearly, that museum too had an interest in the wreck of the Messerschmitt 109 that was quite literally on their doorstep although it was the continued requests by Tony Graves to excavate that ultimately led the farmer to request that the authorities deal with matters.

It was not long before the 590 Explosive Ordnance Disposal Unit of the Royal Engineers (a territorial army unit) had been alerted and tasked with a recovery that might also make for a useful exercise. In due course an official recovery operation was negotiated with the farmer and carried out there during early October 1977, supervised by Captain Spencer Henry. Little of any significance (that is, by way of high-risk) was found in the way of ordnance, save for about five hundred rounds of 7.92mm machine-gun bullets and some

This section of wing fillet jointing strip, found during the recovery operation, bears the unique Werke Nummer of Schelcher's Messerschmitt 109, 1574.

sixty 20mm cannon shells. Ordinarily, such deeply buried ammunition would hardly call for such a large-scale army operation but its purpose as a training exercise was doubtless useful to the TA unit and as a by-product of that exercise it also resulted in the discovery of the pilot's remains. With those remains were found a wallet, some Belgian money and the pilot's decorations. Amongst Schelcher's awards would have been the Spanish Cross in Gold (with swords) for his service with the Legion Condor during the Spanish Civil War. Perhaps one of the most unusual finds was a very large tyre inner tube in the wreckage of the cockpit from either a lorry or aeroplane wheel. Its discovery was something of a mystery, although it was concluded that it must have been some kind of makeshift or improvised survival aid in the event of crashing in the sea. Whilst Luftwaffe pilots obviously had lifejackets, dinghies were not yet standard issue for single-seat fighters operating over Britain. Maybe Schelcher had thought this impromptu piece of kit gave him a little extra security?

Once the TA team had finished their recovery the wreckage was gifted to the Kent Battle of Britain Museum, since relocated from Chilham to Hawkinge. Unfortunately, the museum prohibits the use of cameras or recording equipment of any kind including the taking of notes. Therefore, making any objective observations or the taking of photographs in relation to artefacts displayed from this or other aircraft losses covered within this book is impossible. However, after the site had been cleared by the TA it was visited by at least one other interested party who discovered the pilot's parachute 'D' ring laying on the surface of the field. Nearby were sections of inner wing and parts of the wing/fuselage joint area on a part of which was clearly stamped 1574 – the aircraft Werke Nummer. Some of the wing sections, which would have been in the immediate vicinity of the radiator, had clear impact marks from .303 bullets. Had these also struck the radiator positioned immediately adjacent

Like many families during wartime, the Schelchers endured the loss of two sons, Ekkehard and his brother Roland who was killed and posted missing during 1941 whilst flying a Focke-Wulf Condor over the Atlantic.

The RAF burial party for Oblt Schelcher at Cannock Chase German Military Cemetery in January 1980. Continuing the wartime practice, the RAF have buried their former enemies with full military honours at Cannock when casualties have been found post-war.

Dr Olaf Schelcher and his wife are interviewed for BBC television news at the 1980 funeral ceremony. Closure for another family had been achieved.

to this section of wing then this would have most likely caused the "white smoke" which Plt Off Morton had reported seeing and which was very probably coolant steam.

Although the news media covering the story could not officially name the pilot until formal identification had been established by the British authorities, it had only been during the February of the previous year that the Deutsche Dienstelle in Berlin (the West German military records office) had confirmed in writing to another researcher that this was indeed the crash site of Oblt Ekkehard Schelcher. Berlin went on to state that the pilot had been buried beneath twelve to fifteen feet of soil together with his aircraft and, repeating what the Commonwealth War Graves Commission had earlier stated, added: "According to our records a service was held at the site on Chilham Castle Estate and the site covered over." Notwithstanding this knowledge, the German authorities still regarded the twenty-six-year-old pilot from Plauen to be officially missing. Certainly, he wasn't properly accounted for as far as his family were concerned although unlike all of the other cases covered in this book it might surely be considered that Oblt Schelcher had, until 1977, remained in a recorded field grave which had been hitherto recognised as such by both the British and German authorities. Possibly this was unique amongst the various cases involving missing Luftwaffe aircrew lost over the British Isles.

Like many wartime families, and many covered in this book, the Schelcher family did not just suffer the trauma of losing one son and whilst they were still struggling to come to terms with Ekkehard's disappearance, his brother was also lost whilst flying with the Luftwaffe less than a year later. On 29 April 1941 Oblt Roland Schelcher and his five-man crew were all killed when their Fw 200 Condor was shot down into the sea by flak off the

Shetland Islands. Whilst two bodies of the Condor's crew were eventually recovered Roland's was not one of them. Cruel fate had delivered a double blow to the family with the two eldest sons both missing in action, leaving only one son, Olaf, and a single daughter. Under German rules, Olaf was not permitted active service and was thus fortunate to survive the war eventually becoming a doctor of medicine in the family home of Helmstedt where he was still practicing when news came through about the discovery of his eldest brother, Ekkehard, in late 1977.

From the discovery of Ekkehard Schelcher in 1977 it took until 8 January 1980 before he would finally be buried at Cannock Chase German Military Cemetery. With full military honours, and representatives of the British MOD and German embassy present, Ekkehard was buried in the presence of his younger sibling, Olaf, who finally knew for sure what had happened to at least one of his missing brothers who would now lay in a consecrated military cemetery instead of in a long-forgotten and unmarked field grave.

CHAPTER 5 A Lucky Charm?

WHILST THE EXCAVATION OF a Messerschmitt 109 from where it had crashed at Shuart Farm, St Nicholas at Wade, on the marshy Isle of Thanet, had been undertaken during September 1984, the eventual inquest on the human remains discovered at that time did not take place until July 1986. Coming as it did against the background of an impending Protection of Military Remains Act (which came into force on 9 September 1986) the inquest was the last link in the fascinating chain of events and trail of inquiries which finally led to the identification of the pilot.

During 1975 the Brenzett Aeronautical Museum had conducted what turned out to be an abortive attempt to recover a Messerschmitt 109 from Shuart Farm, St Nicholas at Wade, Kent. Although the operation met with failure, it did succeed in identifying the Werke Nummer of the aeroplane, 3874, which could later be tied into the loss of Uffz Fritz Buchner, shot down on 26 August 1940.

An excavation mounted by the Brenzett Aeronautical Museum during 1975 at this same site did not meet with great success and had to be abandoned due a combination of inclement weather and the inability of the excavator to reach the great depth of the buried wreckage. Before abandonment, however, the site yielded a number of small fragments and a manufacturer's label bearing the number '3874'. From 1975 the site remained undisturbed until it again came under investigation in September 1984, this time by a team led by Peter Dimond and with more fruitful results. Like the previous 'dig', however, the 1984 operation was not without its own problems.

The second and successful excavation on the crash site, led by enthusiast Peter Dimond.

Work began on the excavation early on the morning of Friday 21 September, the Hymac mechanical digger following the course of the previous Brenzett Museum operation. Before too long the maximum range of the excavator's huge boom had been reached and a number of items missed in the previous dig were un-earthed, including a fine example of an MG17 machine gun. Eventually however the depth of the wreckage defeated the mechanical excavator and, additionally, technical difficulties prevented an extension arm being fitted onto its hydraulic jib thus resulting in the suspension of operations until a larger machine could be brought to the site on the following day.

With the arrival of the second machine there was some success in enlarging what was already an enormous hole until finally the bulk of the crumpled wreckage was revealed at a staggering depth of thirty-five feet, although when the digging was eventually forced to stop at around forty feet no trace of the engine had been found. Quite likely this was the deepest excavation ever carried out to recover a buried World War Two fighter wreck, and is illustrative of the astonishing depth to which a crashing aircraft can penetrate the soil. At something in excess of forty feet the excavation had become very unstable and hazardous with the sides collapsing and water now flooding into the bottom of the hole which, of course, was well below sea level on this coastal marsh location. The concertinaed wreckage was found compacted into the last few feet of the excavation, and apart from a tailwheel and crumpled fuselage panels, much of the cockpit area was also uncovered in this compressed mass. It was whilst the recovery team sorted this part of the wreckage that the remains of the pilot came to light. Immediately operations were halted and the police duly summoned and in the now gathering darkness Police Constables Brown and Atkinson of the Kent Constabulary arrived on the scene. Acting in his capacity as coroner's officer, PC Atkinson took charge of the remains – albeit that he was rather nonplussed by the rather unusual situation that had been presented to him. Casualties from the war were clearly not on his normal caseload.

Those involved with the excavation had long previously concluded that the pilot must have been Unteroffizier Fritz Buchner of 6/JG3 based upon a process of elimination in respect of losses sustained on 26 August 1940. That process had already established the crash date from local and RAF reports and although no definite proof of identity had been seen amongst the remains handed to the police, there had been a tunic collar bearing the rank marking of an Unteroffizier and a torn handkerchief with the initials 'FB' embroidered in red into one corner. This would certainly seem to point towards Fritz Buchner. The Werke Nummer of the aeroplace was also discovered on several makers labels and confirmed the 3874 number already ascertained by the Brenzett team. Unfortunately, this number was not sufficient evidence alone for identification as the aeroplane serials and pilots' names were not recorded together in Luftwaffe loss returns. Further clues, however, were subsequently discovered amongst the wreckage. Traces of yellow fuselage bar were found which indicated a II Gruppe machine (to which the 6th Staffel belonged) and also the remains of an emblem of II/JG3 in the form of a black/white segmented shield bordered with red. Most significant, however, was

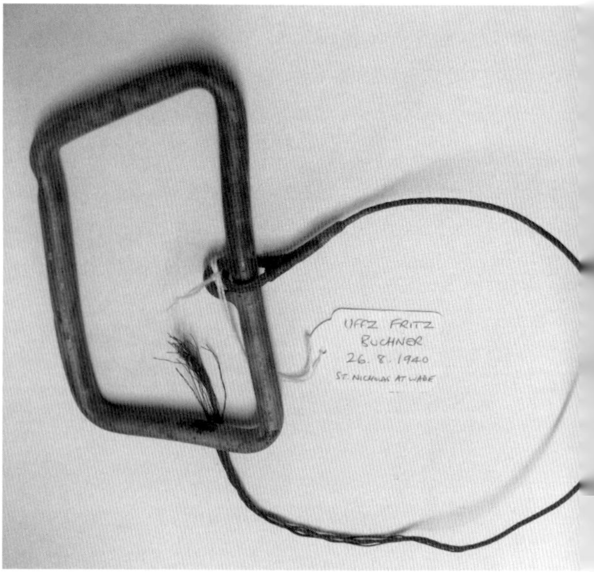

The parachute 'D' ring was proof enough that the pilot of this aeroplane had not escaped before it had crashed.

Uffz Fritz Buchner poses for a studio portrait photograph as the archetypal Luftwaffe fighter pilot.

a small lucky charm in the form of a cloverleaf with a red ladybird superimposed. The reverse was engraved with the name Christ'l and the date 4.4.1940. According to German records this would have been Fritz Buchner's 24th birthday, he having been born in Augsburg on 4 April, 1916, a child of the First World War. This additional information was passed to the authorities by a recovery team now wholly confident that sufficient evidence existed to provide an early and simple identification of the pilot as Fritz Buchner. However, this was not to be and protracted enquiries by both the British and German authorities

Amongst artefacts recovered during the 1984 excavation was this handkerchief with the embroidered initials FB, a find which helped to identify the pilot.

Clinching the pilot's identity was a tiny lucky charm inscribed with the name of Fritz Buchner's girlfriend and the date of his birthday. Of itself it was a remarkably lucky find!

continued over almost two years before an inquest was finally held to consider all of the evidence.

This was held by HM Coroner Rebecca Cobb at Pierrepoint Hall, Broadstairs, on 1 July 1986 after both official and unofficial efforts had been made to track down additional evidence. In the interim period, however the German War Graves Service had pre-empted any coroner's decision by stating in a letter dated 20 March, 1985 that the remains were to be interred at Cannock Chase as those of an unknown airman. Evidently, the German authorities were, for some reason, unhappy to accept the remains as those of Fritz Buchner. The recovery team, anxious that Buchner should not be denied burial under a named headstone, redoubled their efforts to track down his family in Germany. Letters to the family home in 1940 at Lorenz-Holkeplats II, Augsburg, only drew the response 'Not known at this address' but careful research identified Frau Emma Heumos, then living in an Augsburg old peoples' home, as Fritz Buchner's sister and his sole surviving close relative.

This information gleaned from the Augsburg register of inhabitants was passed to the S10 (Air) Branch of the Ministry of Defence on 27 March 1985, with the suggestion that an official approach to this lady might well elicit relevant information. Instead, the MoD stated that there was absolutely no official interest in following up this line of inquiry but if the recovery team wished to contact Frau Heumos direct then there would be no objection to this. Clearly, if any progress was going to be made in the case then the recovery team's researchers would have to go it alone. Contact was duly made and resulted in information which, in the event, proved more than invaluable when the inquest opened in 1986. It was neither the first time nor the last that those involved with such recoveries had questioned or challenged a call made by either coroner or other authorities and, in this case, it would enable formal identification to be confirmed.

Opening the formal proceedings HM Coroner announced that this was an inquest into the death of a person who may have been Friedrich (Fritz) Johann Buchner. In total, six witnesses were called to give evidence and the first was PC Brian Atkinson who had been the coroner's officer at the time of the 1984 excavation. PC Atkinson described how he had collected the human remains from Shuart Farm in a large box at 7.30p.m. on Saturday, 22 September 1984, and subsequently deposited them in Margate Public Mortuary. It was here on Monday 24 September that he examined the remains and retrieved a number of items which were presented to the coroner in evidence. These were the eagle and swastika from the pilot's badge, a uniform tunic collar, a piece of canvas bearing ink writing and a handkerchief showing the initials FB. These became exhibits C2, C3, C4 and C5 respectively. Another article was also shown to PC Atkinson (Exhibit C1) which he identified as an aircraft label given to him with the remains by Peter Dimond. It bore the markings : 'BFW 109E-1 18/3874'. In 1985 PC Atkinson stood down as coroner's officer, and on 11 June 1985 he identified the remains on hand-over to the new coroner's officer, PC Wiggins, at Margate Hospital Mortuary where they were then being kept.

The next witness called was PC Nigel Douglas who described how he visited the site on Monday 24 September as a result of his personal interest in the subject. Whilst there he discovered the II/JG3 squadron emblem on a fuselage panel lying alongside the still open but water-logged excavation. He also told that he had spoken with an elderly gentleman who was brought to the site by Mr Tapp, the farmer on whose land the aircraft had crashed. PC Douglas told the court that this man, a retired agricultural worker at Shuart Farm, had described seeing the crash during the August of 1940. Whilst he did not remember the exact date, or even the day of the week, he was adamant that it had happened during the month of August and said that it had come down from very high altitude, diving under full power. PC Douglas said that the witness was quite specific that no one had baled out. Douglas then went on to describe his own researches at the Public Record Office (now The National Archives) in Kew into the background of this incident. There, he had examined the records of 56 Squadron, North Weald, and had established that their Hurricanes were in combat with Me 109s at the relevant time and place on 26 August 1940.

Having taken evidence from PC Douglas, who had not been acting in his official capacity as a police officer, the coroner then went on to admit the written evidence of 81-year-old John Marsh, a retired agricultural worker of The Street, St Nicholas at Wade, who when interviewed on 20 June 1986, had provided the following short statement:

> "In 1940 I was a baker. I was allowed to take food and cigarettes to the troops stationed in the area and during August of that year I remember a Messerschmitt crashing. No parachute came down and it dived into the ground at Shuart's Farm, just leaving its mark on the surface."

Next to be called was Flight Lieutenant David Carroll of RAF Manston. Being fluent in German he first provided translation of the Luftwaffe Verlustmeldung which detailed the losses of II Gruppe JG3 for 26 August 1940. Most of the facts were self-explanatory, detailing name, rank, staffel, age, service number, birthplace, etc. The wording across columns 15 to 18 of that document was translated as reading: 'Further whereabouts not known'. Flight Lieutenant Carroll then went on to say that he understood the aircraft had been partially excavated by the Brenzett Aeronautical Museum in 1975, at which time the cockpit had been uncovered and "the remains of the pilot seen in the wreckage". He then confirmed that at the request of the MoD and German authorities the site had been filled in and left. Although this was accepted as sworn evidence and not challenged, this record is firmly and quite rightly denied by those who were then involved with the Brenzett group.

Indeed, that denial was borne out by the findings of the 1984 dig which revealed quite clearly that the 1975 operation had come nowhere near to uncovering the wreckage or even getting anywhere close to it. And neither had it been filled in at the request of the authorities. The suggestions that "...the remains of the pilot had been seen in the wreckage" are fanciful to say the very least. Quite simply, it would have been impossible during that 1975 dig. However, Carroll was later emphatic about what he had said; whatever the truth of the matter he had been informed that the MOD here, and also the authorities in Bonn, had certainly asked the Brenzett team to leave the site undisturbed in the future. That, though, was a long way from the remains having earlier been seen in the wreckage. It is clear, however, that officially there had been no interest in or support for any moves that might do the right thing by this missing pilot and his family. Although the German authorities over the years have generally shown a far more positive attitude to the discovery and naming of missing casualties, it is certainly the case that the MOD in the UK have consistently been opposed to such work. That is notwithstanding the overwhelmingly favourable response from families of missing aircrew when they are eventually found.

Flight Lieutenant Carroll's evidence then turned to the items found in the wreckage. First under scrutiny was a piece of cloth or canvas which he described as being "possibly a portion of Mae West". It bore lettering in ink which when translated read, 'I Bty., Light Flak Regiment 22', beneath which was a sewn-on linen tab bearing the name Zeiche or Zelker. This was taken to be a German surname. Beside this apparent surname the inscription which attributed the item to 'I Bty., Light Flak Regiment 22' was repeated. David Carroll then expounded to the court his theory over this item. Assuming it to be a piece of Mae West (perhaps wrongly) he suggested that it had been issued to Zeiche/Zelker for use in the projected cross-Channel invasion, Operation Sealion. This man, he assumed, had been a friend of Fritz Buchner and had loaned him his Mae West. Why this should have been at all necessary when lifejackets were part of the standard equipment issued to all Luftwaffe aircrew was not explained to the court. Furthermore, just about all of the pilot's Mae West had been retained by the recovery group and had not been amongst the items handed to the authorities as being in any way significant to the inquiry. If the item that Carroll had referred to was indeed part of the pilot's lifejacket then the more likely explanation is that it had been first used by another serviceman, returned to stores and then issued to this pilot.

Exhibit C7 was then examined and this was described as a piece of paper bearing the words 'Fur verwunden, Wolhausen A.G. Berlin' which was explained to be a first aid dressing pack cover. Also presented was a Luftwaffe shirt collar bearing the label 'St Mauritain, Paris 27, Bld des Capucines', which was presumably the name of the maker. Neither the first aid dressing nor the shirt collar bore any significance in the task of identifying the airman. However, the handkerchief, which was also shown to Flight Lieutenant Carroll, most certainly did have considerable significance. The red initials F.B. were now becoming more and more firmly established in the minds of those present at the court as

Plt Off Kenneth Marston, a Hurricane pilot with 56 Squadron, can be identified as Fritz Buchner's victor. Marston was killed in a flying accident on 14 December 1940.

incontrovertible evidence that the pilot was indeed Fritz Buchner; but David Carroll's evidence was not yet complete. Serving as he did at RAF Manston, the nearest RAF station, he had in effect been co-opted to assist the local civilian police with their investigations into the death of this German airman and he clearly threw himself into the task with considerable personal enthusiasm and interest.

From the Air Historical Branch of the MoD he explained that he had secured an intelligence report of 56 Squadron for 26 August 1940. This described how that squadron had left North Weald at 11.49 hours to patrol Maidstone at 12,000 feet. They were then diverted to Hawkinge at 15,000 feet, where they encountered twelve Dornier Do 215s [almost certainly Do 17s] and 30 Me 109s and He 113s (sic). The fighters were in groups of six, line astern. First the formation flew westwards and then turned south east. Pilot Officer Marston destroyed two Me 109s. He hit the port wing and radiator of one, attacking from port astern, and sent it diving into the clouds. Pilot Officer Marston saw the pilot "trying to get out" of his Messerschmitt but when he came out of the cloud he saw the wreckage burning in a crater two miles south west of Westgate; a location which corresponds almost exactly with Shuart Farm, St Nicholas at Wade. Pilot Officer Marston then saw another Me 109 which he dived on and opened fire from seventy yards, sending it down to crash one hundred yards behind a Defiant of 264 Squadron that had crash-landed five miles south of Reculver. Yet another 109 was sent into the sea by Pilot Officer M H Mounsdon near Whitstable. According to 56 Squadron's report all the Me 109s had 'Yellow markings round the fuselage crosses'. (Author: Probably the yellow fuselage numerals and gruppen 'bar' markings) The report went on to add that Red 2, Pilot Officer Wicks, had baled out near Canterbury and Green 2, Sergeant Smythe, had force-landed at Rochford following this action.

Flight Lieutenant Carroll had come to the conclusion that the second Messerschmitt claimed by 56 Squadron had been that of Unteroffizier Willy Finke of 4./JG3, which in fact crashed at Grays Farm, Reculver, killing its pilot. The third, which went into the sea, had been flown by Unteroffizier Emil Müller of the 4th Staffel. His body was later found at sea, but not recovered. Thus all three men appeared together on the same Verlustmeldung for JG3 and were recorded as lost in the area of Canterbury whilst flying a fighter cover mission for bombers. On the documentary evidence alone, said David Carroll, it could be concluded as at least an eighty per cent certainty that the aeroplane at Shuart Farm was that flown by Fritz Buchner. The coroner then asked him what he felt of the possibility it were Fritz Buchner taking the documentary *and* physical evidence into account. His reply was that, in his view, this increased the probability to a certainty. Before releasing him as a witness the coroner asked him one further question, the significance of which became obvious later: "May you help me with the German word Braut?" she asked him. He replied that this was a colloquial German word meaning the same as 'Frau' in grammatical German, and although not necessarily indicating marital status, a literal translation would be 'bride'.

PC Wiggins then told how Dr. P J O'Donnell, consultant pathologist, had been handed the remains for examination. Subsequently, however, in October 1984, PC Wiggins had been told by the MoD that doubts had been raised by the German authorities as to the possible identification of the deceased and as a result, he set out trying to locate the grave of an unknown German said to exist at St Nicholas at Wade. Although not mentioned in PC Wiggins' evidence, this question had been no doubt raised by entry 1647 on a list of those German burials in the United Kingdom not in the Cannock Chase German Military Cemetery, drawn up by the German War Graves Service in 1982. The entry reads: 'Ein Unbekannter Soldat 26.08.40 St Nicholas at Wade, Kent'.

PC Wiggins described how he had scoured cemeteries and burial records at Monkton, Margate, St Nicholas at Wade and other locations in the Thanet area, but could find no trace of the alleged burial. The records of Messrs Bernard Cole (undertakers) of Aylesham were also examined but threw no light at all on the mystery; neither did the burials at Cannock Chase cemetery throw up any possible links to the reported St Nicholas at Wade grave. In fact, the 1982 listing may well have been an oblique reference to the Shuart Farm crash site since the location, provisionally identified by the Brenzett team as the likely last resting place of Fritz Buchner, had already been notified to the German authorities by the Brenzett Museum after their abortive 1975 recovery. All along, PC Wiggins had probably been looking for a non-existent local grave and was unaware that this reference had related instead to the actual crash site!

On 24 January 1986, a post-mortem was held on the remains by Dr O'Donnell who reported on 17 April that they consisted of fragmentary human bones from most parts of the body with the exception of any skull, facial bones or teeth. The identification of vertebrae and pelvic bones proved, said Dr O'Donnell, that the remains constituted a body as such, for without the spine or pelvis independent human life could not be sustained.

Peter Dimond, who had been the nominal leader of the recovery team, then gave evidence to the court and told how the wreckage had been excavated from around thirty feet and that once human remains were identified the police were called to the scene. The first officer to arrive was PC Brown, who went to the crater and surveyed the scene, leaving PC Atkinson to take charge of the remains. He then went on to explain how the lucky charm clover leaf medallion had later turned up amongst the wreckage and, realising its significance, this had been handed over to the coroner's officer. In his letter of 14 December 1985, Peter Dimond had asked Frau Heumos about the medallion and had sent her an enlarged photograph of it. In a reply dated 9 April 1986 Emma Heumos's son, Günther, writing on her behalf, provided the confirmation which had long been sought. A translation of the letter was read to the court by the coroner:

"Dear Mr Dimond,

"I, Günther Heumos, am writing on behalf of my eighty-year-old mother, Emma Heumos, the last surviving sister of the crashed pilot, Fritz Buchner.

"There is no doubt that the body is that of Fritz Buchner. He has been described as missing since August 1940. The information from the German air force is as follows: did not return from active flight over England. My mother also confirms that his bride was called Christl and that he received the medallion on his twenty-fourth birthday, 4 April 1940.

"Mr Dimond, I do not know how I can thank you for all your careful and difficult research. Perhaps I can be permitted as a token of my appreciation to offer you two photographs of the pilot and a metal decorative wall plaque from Augsburg, his place of birth.

"A photocopy of my mother's birth certificate and a photocopy of my uncle's birth certificate are enclosed in order to prove the relationship to Fritz Buchner.With many thanks for all your trouble.

Yours sincerely

Günther Heumos"

The last person to be called to give evidence was Philip Powell, representing MoD S10 (Air). He told the court that he had been involved in the general background of the whole affair and introduced a number of relevant points. He confirmed from his contact with the German Embassy in London that the name Fritz was an abbreviation of the name Friedrich. He then went on to explain that the apparently spurious name and unit marked on what was thought to be a part of Mae West was the main reason for the German authorities being unhappy about the identification of Buchner. However, it was Mr Powell's view that this item of equipment, whatever it had been, had previously been issued to a man named Zieche or Zelker of 1 Bty, Light Fak Regt 22, before being returned to stores and re-issued to Uffz Buchner. (Author: This view conformed to that taken by the recovery team). He further went on to state that the ministry were happy that this man was Buchner, but added that no embarrassment would be caused either way if he were named or declared unidentified. He also confirmed that following inquiries made via the German Embassy, the MOD were satisfied that Fritz Buchner was unmarried. Christl, he therefore concluded, was his fiancée. His final comments related to the conduct of the dig and MoD policy and guidelines on aircraft recovery, and whilst confirming there was no legal requirement to obtain permission for such excavations from the MOD he added that "... this was the usual and accepted custom and practice". In this case, he told the court, no permission had been sought of the ministry and none had been given.

In her summing up, the coroner described how the inquest had posed many problems. First, she had to be satisfied that there was a body lying within the area of her jurisdiction. Shuart Farm met this criteria, but did the remains constitute a body? Dr O'Donnell's evidence had confirmed this to be so and therefore it was just a matter of identification. Considerable time and effort she said had been taken both officially and unofficially by those involved in the case, and she placed on record her thanks to all those who had helped and to those who had assisted as witnesses and with background information, praising their "enthusiasm and knowledge". In closing the inquest, which had lasted three hours, she concluded with the following statement:

'I do find the evidence both sufficient and convincing to name this man as Friedrich Johann Buchner who was a corporal in the Luftwaffe and that he was born on 4 April 1916 in Augsburg and died on 26 August 1940, at or in the sky above Shuart Farm, St Nicholas at Wade, Kent, aged twenty-four years. I am not certain of his marital status,

Fritz Buchner poses with his Messerschmitt 109 whilst he was serving with JG 27. It was this aircraft, his lucky number 12, that Fritz was flying on one occasion when he experienced oxygen equipment failure. He wrote of this terrifying event in a letter home to his parents.

> but I am more convinced than not that he was unmarried. The clinical cause of death is unascertainable, but I do find from the evidence of eyewitnesses and various records, most particularly the report of 56 Squadron, that Friedrich Johann Buchner, otherwise known as Fritz Buchner, was killed in action during World War 2. Although that is not one of the findings normally recommended in the coroner's court rules, it is the verdict I return on a case which I have found most interesting. Again, I thank all those whose help led to this most satisfactory conclusion."

Speaking after the inquest, Flt Lt Carroll said: "Over the last two years I have grown quite close to Fritz Buchner. He fought a brave battle and he died honourably. He deserved a proper burial, not one as an un-named airman."

So it was that the saga of Fritz Buchner drew almost to a close more than forty-four years after the violent crash that had driven Mersserschmitt 3874 deep into Kentish marshland entombing its young pilot. After the passage of a further two years and following extensive investigations an inquest had been held and a conclusion reached which was to the satisfaction of the MOD, family and the recovery team. However, there can be no doubting the fact that had the recovery team not pressed on with their determination to find the pilot's family in Germany then Fritz Buchner would have gone to a grave at Cannock Chase marked as that of an unknown airman. The key to the mystery had surely been the name and date on a tiny medallion, discovered some while after the dig, and the team's success in tracking down the Buchner family. Until events eventually unfolded as they did in 1986 the family had heard nothing since II/JG 3's Oblt Erich Woitke had written to Fritz Buchner's parents on 31 August 1940. Woitke had led II Gruppe during the operation when Fritz had been lost and he also managed to down one Spitfire (sic) during that sortie, although his victim had probably been a 56 Squadron Hurricane flown by Plt Off Bryan Wicks. In his letter to Frau and Herr Buchner he wrote:

Fritz Buchner's dog, Peterle, often flew with his master in a Messerschmitt 109. According to family members Peterle actually flew on some operational flights over Britain!

"On 26 August I took my group over Great Britain and we were advancing against southern England when I think your son probably suffered some damage to his engine. This made an emergency landing on the other side of the Channel necessary.

I don't think you should make too much about the safety of your son as he was a skilled pilot and our expectation is that he can take care of himself. We all hope that he made an emergency landing safely and think that with his excellent flying skills he will have managed that easily.

Of course, once I have any further information I will notify you at once.

Yours truly,

Woitke"

Of their son's flying skill and ability to survive, the Buchners had no doubt. Not many months previously he had written to them:

"Yesterday I was a bit unlucky. Hostile aeroplanes were reported at high altitude and my Leutnant flew with me. From the height of 5,000 metres one has to breathe by oxygen.

I switched mine on and we continued to climb to 8,000 metres. Unfortunately I didn't know that the tube must have been squeezed and I didn't get enough oxygen. After about twenty minutes everything went black and I lost consciousness. Literally, I was totally gone. When I woke up again I was at 4,000 metres going straight down. That means that my aircraft, good old number '12' had saved me. I don't know how I came down. I was very lucky. Anyone else would have definitely been dead."

Despite his earlier survivor's luck, and Erich Woitke's reassurances, we now know that the promised and hoped-for further information would not be forthcoming for another forty-six years. Meanwhile, the Buchner family had gone on with their lives – his parents wondering and hoping for some news for many years after the war. On a daily basis they had an ever-present reminder of their son in the presence of his little dog, Peterle, who had been sent home to them from Fritz's airfield in France. Peterle, who survived until 1950, had been the faithful companion of Fritz and had flown with him on numerous occasions in his Messerschmitt 109.

Master and faithful friend. Here, Fritz Buchner is seen in the cockpit of a Messerschmitt 109 with his pet dog.

The final act in the saga of Fritz Buchner was his burial with full military honours at Cannock Chase German Military Cemetery on 8 May 1987 with members of his family following Fritz's coffin to its last resting place. Writing to the author in July of that year, family member Helmut Dumberger noted:

"The recovery team have enabled Fritz to have an honourable burial and for us to know where he is and exactly what happened to him. It is a pity that his parents had not lived to see this. I can absolutely assure you it is what they would have wanted for their boy. We must thank everyone who made this possible, and feel that we should also offer these thanks on behalf of our Fritz who would surely be grateful for all the efforts made on his account. His lucky charm had not been so lucky for poor Fritz in the way that he had imagined, although many years later it would turn out very fortunate indeed that he had been carrying it that day."

CHAPTER 6 5 September 1940 to 5 September 1986

WITH THE DISCOVERY OF Unteroffizier Fritz Buchner's remains at St Nicholas at Wade, Kent, in 1984 it appeared almost certain that the last of all the missing Luftwaffe Me 109 pilots from the Battle of Britain who had fallen on British soil had been found. Indeed, with Buchner's inquest on I July 1986 it seemed more than positive that no more missing Luftwaffe pilots from this period would be found (unless accidentally) prior to the impending introduction of the Protection of Military Remains Act on 9 September of that year. Even if there were any others left to discover then the Ministry of Defence would almost certainly refuse the granting of a recovery licence in respect of such sites as required under the provisions of the new legislation. It was a surprise, therefore, when aviation archaeologist Andrew Cresswell discovered the remains of another Luftwaffe pilot in the wreckage of his Messerschmitt 109 near Appledore railway station in Kent just four days before the act came into force. The surprise was considerable, particularly as the site had previously been the subject of a major investigation during the early 1970s by local enthusiast Eric Boswell who had carried out what seemed to have been an extensive excavation although he did not report the finding of any human remains at the site. Boswell, however, had later passed many of his finds to the Brenzett Aeronatical Museum.

Andrew Cresswell's interest came about through discovering from a colleague who had driven the JCB excavator on the first dig at the site, that numerous items of wreckage were not removed from the hole, and that quite probably more parts of the aircraft were deeper still and had possibly not even been disturbed. Andrew's intention, therefore, was to re-excavate the site in order hopefully to solve the mystery of what had happened to the pilot who was thought to be Lt Helmut Strobl, lost there on 5 September 1940. He was joined on this project by a number of the more active aviation archaeologists of the period in what would be the second excavation on 5 September 1986: coincidentally the anniversary of the crash.

Excavations down to a depth of twelve to fourteen feet revealed sundry items, but little of great interest, yet an intriguing and most unexpected find came to light in the form of the control column grip; the Brenzett Aeronautical Museum already having had on display a control column top attributed to this same aeroplane. With that discovery there was some momentary doubt about the history of the site being excavated. Was it, in fact, the same

Lt Helmut Strobl poses with his Messerschmitt 109. Born on 5 September he was shot down and killed on 5 September. Many years later his body would be discovered on 5 September and, ultimately, buried on 5 September.

site excavated years earlier by the Ashford and Tenterden team? Just to augment that confusion there was also a duplicated air intelligence report which could well have perhaps added some weight to those doubts. The first report describes a Messerschmitt 109 down on 5 September 1940 as having 'crashed one mile east of Appledore, Kent, at 1650 hours on 5/9/40. Fitted with DB601A engine, aircraft crashed following fighter action. Was completely destroyed and burnt out. Armament and armour standard. Pilot dead.'

The second report gives a location which coincides roughly with the position of the crash site under investigation and stated as having crashed one mile east of Appledore, although it is timed at one hour earlier. The report reads: 'Crashed one mile south west (sic) of Snargate, in the Marshes at 1550 hours on 5/9/40. Identification marking not visible but plate found was marked "BFW 109, Nr. 302, Regensburg 3836/12". Cause of crash unknown, but aircraft dived into ground and wreckage lies completely buried in a deep crater.' (The reference to 'south west' is probably a mistake on the original report and most likely should have read north west.) Clearly this report related to Leutnant Strobl's aeroplane. Extensive research, however, has failed to identify any other crash in the locality on this day which could account for both reports and it was concluded therefore that only one incident had actually occurred; this being the loss of Helmut Strobl of 5./JG 27 in a crash south of Appledore station, and at a point some yards east of the B2080 Appledore to Brenzett road.

Andrew Cresswell's dig on the crash site of Helmut Strobl's aircraft at Appledore, Kent, on 5 September 1986.

Whilst doubts were initially raised about the control column, these were quickly dispelled by the discovery of bottles and food wrappers that can only have been discarded by Eric Boswell's team well over ten years earlier. Apart from the control column grip other major finds included a flare pistol and the main aircraft constructor's plate confirming the Werke Nummer to be 3627 and the aeroplane in which Strobl had been flying when he was recorded as lost. At this depth, however, human remains also came to light together with items of flying clothing and equipment; a torn uniform jacket, a pair of flying boots, the remnants of a pair of Luftwaffe riding breeches, and torn shreds of a parachute. Worryingly, these were found stuffed inside a plastic farm fertilizer sack. The most significant discovery amongst these articles, however, was an identity disc bearing the number 53537/4, positive proof that the remains were indeed those of Leutnant Helmut Thomas Strobl. Further personal effects which came to light included a small medallion, some coins, and a green and white handkerchief marked with the inscription 'II 27', which was taken to indicate II./JG 27 – Strobl's Gruppe with JG 27. The remains, together with the means of identity, were immediately reported to the authorities and handed to Police Constable Stevens of the Kent Police force from Lydd who attended the site that afternoon.

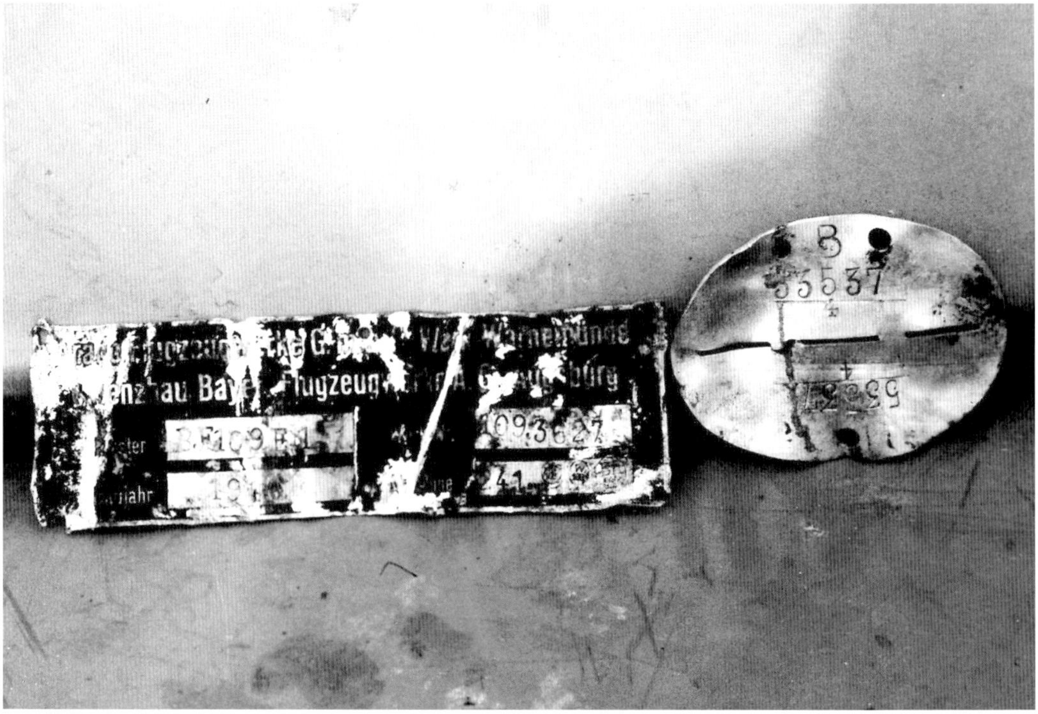

During the 1986 excavation the pilot's identity disc was discovered providing positive proof as to who he was. With the disc was also found the aircraft's main construction plate marked with the Werke Nummer of the Messerschmitt 109 that Strobl had been lost in, 3627.

Whilst the remains had been positively identified, albeit not yet formally, there still remained the mystery of the relics attributed to Strobl's aircraft which in the light of the subsequent discoveries in 1986 were clearly not from the same aeroplane! It was eventually concluded that the provenance of items of wreckage from *three* Messerschmitt 109s excavated at about the same time by Eric Boswell must have subsequently become confused. These were Strasser's aeroplane (7/JG 52 1.9.1940), Volk's (9/JG 53 11.11,1940) and Strobl's. *(Coincidentally, in the case of Josef Volk's aeroplane another discrepancy in terms of relics attributed to it and items which had been displayed at Brenzett Museum was uncovered with the re-excavation of that site in 1984 when the propeller hub was found – an item already attributed as being on display at Brenzett. Clearly, there must be serious question marks placed on the historical veracity of some artefacts and their associated histories then displayed there).* However, the duplicated control column originally on display at Brenzett could not have originated from the Volk aeroplane either, since part of that control column was found on the 1984 re-excavation of the crash site. In view of the fact that no control column existed in the display of items from Strasser's aeroplane it can only be deduced that this is where the item probably originated.

Nevertheless, none of this helped take forward the investigations into the loss of Helmut Strobl and his aeroplane, although it did throw serious question marks over the efficacy of earlier recoveries. The provenance of the other relics displayed from Strobl's aeroplane must therefore be questionable, although it is highly probable that at least the parachute release

Helmut Strobl had previously been shot down during the French campaign but had managed to make a successful forced-landing. He poses here with his aircraft and a group of German infantrymen.

On 5 September 1940, Lt Strobl had been shot down by Sgt Alex Hurry in a Tangmere-based Hurricane of 43 Squadron. Hurry is photographed here later in the war when flying Spitfires.

buckle displayed at Brenzett was from Strobl's aeroplane since the others, Volk and Strasser, did not involve casualties and thus there would have been no parachutes in those wrecks. Nor can there be any doubt as to the origins of the Iron Cross First Class which is known to have been found on the first excavation at Appledore and which had been clearly unpinned from the uniform tunic that had then been stuffed back into the buried plastic bag. This medal is apparently now displayed at the Kent Battle of Britain Museum collection, Hawkinge according to published sources.

Helmut Thomas Strobl's remains had been found on 5 September. He had also been shot down on 5 September and, by strange coincidence, he was born on 5 September, 1915. His parents, Thomas and Maria, lived at Kolbnitz, in Molltall, Austria, although Helmut was born in Spittal, Drau. After attending elementary school in Kolbnitz, Helmut went to the secondary school in Klagenfurt where he took his 'Abitur', roughly equivalent to today's GCSE A Level. Whilst still at school he developed a deep interest in gliding and went on to earn certificates in the sport at Wasserkuppe auf der Rohn and later qualifying as a gliding instructor at Gaissberg, near Salzburg. After school his intention was to study aeronautical engineering but as no courses were available in his native Austria he emigrated to Germany on the condition that he complete his military service in Austria. After infantry training from September 1936 to October 1939 he trained as a pilot at Talerhof airfield near Graz, and was then sent to the Militarakedemie at Wiener-Neustadt on 1 October, 1937. He then graduated through one other training school and an officer cadet college where he was awarded his pilot's qualification badge on 4 May, 1939 before being transferred to his first operational unit, JG 3, at Merseburg on 7 December but was subsequently posted to JG 27 on 1 February, 1940. It was with this unit's 5th Staffel that he made his last flight on his twenty-fifth birthday as part of a bomber escort mission over southern England.

From examination of reports by RAF squadrons involved in that action over Kent it is clear that Helmut Strobl fell victim to the guns of Sergeant L Hurry in Hurricane P3386 of 43 Squadron, RAF Tangmere. In his combat report 'Alex' Hurry sets out concise details of the battle which undoubtedly confirm him as the victor:

> "I was flying in Blue Section as Blue 3 at 20,000 feet over Biggin Hill when Blue 1 turned and dived. I followed but lost him in thick haze and joined up with Blue 2 at 10,000 feet and climbed again to rejoin the squadron. At 18,000 feet at 1605 hours over Maidstone I sighted some 30-40 Me 109s heading WNW at 15,000 feet. I climbed into the sun and gave the 'Tally Ho!' then turned and dived on the rear vic of five enemy aircraft. During my dive they turned south and I carried out a quarter attack on the outer aircraft. Length of burst about 5 seconds. Enemy aircraft half rolled and dived and I followed as the remaining four enemy aircraft were turning to attack me. Enemy aircraft pulled out at 5,000 feet and flew south. I caught him again 12 miles NW of Dungeness and fired a burst of 6 seconds. He caught fire, half rolled and dived vertically into the ground near Appledore Station about 10 miles NW of Dungeness. No attempt was made at evasion. Enemy markings: Dull green with white wingtips. Silver (sic) undersurfaces. I did not see the pilot bale out. Weather: Hazy with 4/10 Cloud at 17,000 feet. Visibility 12 miles."

(Author's Note: By coincidence, it is now clear that on 8 August 1940 Strobl and Hurry had previously met in combat off the Isle of Wight during actions over Convoy CW9 Peewit. During that action, Sgt Hurry's Hurricane had been hit and damaged. An account of this action is contained in *Convoy Peewit*, by this author, and published by Grub Street in 2010).

Whilst Sergeant Hurry's facts fit exactly and very neatly with the known circumstances of Helmut Strobl's crash, the letter home to his parents sent by the deputy Staffelführer, Oberleutnant Erwin Daig, was rather less definite and unfortunately gave the Strobl family false hope that he may yet be alive and prisoner of war. Writing on 8 September Daig said:

> "I must, even though it is very difficult for me, write to you officially at this time. I am writing as the Deputy Staffelführer and I must inform you that Helmut has gone missing during action over England. It is very, very bitter; not only for you but also for all of us here.
>
> "On 5 September 1940, his birthday, we took off to accompany bombers who were to attack an airfield south of London in the vicinity of Maidstone. At about midday, on the way back, Helmut was suddenly attacked from behind by an English fighter which no one had seen and which then immediately dived away. Helmut also dived down and then went into a glide with a plume of smoke coming from his engine. Four aircraft of another Gruppe circled round over him. We are all of the opinion that he crash-landed in England and has been taken prisoner. If he was wounded then it must surely not have been fatal. I am not telling you this just to comfort you, but because this actually fits the facts, although of course I cannot guarantee it.
>
> "Helmut was for all of us one of our best comrades; one who without saying much held his head high and always did his duty to the very best of his ability. His loss has been felt greatly by everyone. It is to be hoped that he will come back after the war. If he has been taken prisoner it will be some time before he can give any information. His things will be sent on to you. There are some films in the package which have not yet been developed.
>
> "There is not much more for me to say except that the Staffel expresses its sympathy to you, as I do my own, and there is still the hope that he will return. And now, my best wishes to you.
>
> From Erwin Daig."

The day after Erwin Daig had written this letter he was himself shot down over England and taken prisoner at Storrington in West Sussex and it then fell to somebody else to write a very similar letter home to Daig's family. Unfortunately, Erwin Daig was not destined to find his erstwhile comrade-in-arms, Helmut Strobl, amongst the faces of his fellow prisoners as he must have surely hoped.

Some months after the discovery at Appledore, a formal inquest was opened by HM Coroner at Ashford at which Andrew Cresswell and the author were required to attend in order to give evidence, both oral and documentary. First, Superintendent Rickwood of the Kent Police at Folkestone gave evidence as to the police involvement in the discovery and stated that from information received an assumption had been made as to the pilot's identity and went on to add that he hoped this assumption would be borne out through evidence that would be presented to the court. Giving evidence as to the background of his excavation, Andrew Cresswell explained that he had excavated down to a depth of twenty feet and then went on to explain how the dig had been conducted and why. Taking matters further, the coroner asked how the remains had been discovered to which Andrew replied that they had been found inside a plastic bag. Although this fact had been clearly known to the coroner already it was nevertheless a shocking revelation to those assembled in the court room. When the bag was found, Andrew told how it was investigated by the recovery team who were shocked to discover that it contained substantial human remains, including flying clothing and a pair of flying boots along with an identity disc. Consequently, the police were immediately called to the scene and the recovery halted. Following Andrew's evidence, the author was called and told the court about his research work that had tracked down the Strobl family and others who had been flying with Helmut on the fateful day.

At the end of proceedings the coroner pronounced: "I am satisfied that these were the remains of Lt Helmut Strobl who met his death at or near Appledore on 5 September 1940. Thanks must go to Mr Cresswell for making this discovery and to Mr Saunders for his research work which included finding the pilot's relatives. However, I must say a few words about the earlier investigation. It would seem that these remains were the subject of that recovery team's discovery, since the plastic bag in which they were found could not have been in existence at the time of the crash. I am disappointed that a proper report of that discovery was not made and find the actions of those unknown persons to have been utterly reprehensible. It must go on record, however, that the subsequent actions of Mr Cresswell and Mr Saunders have helped bring about a satisfactory conclusion to this sad case."

As previously explained, this earlier recovery was led by a Mr Eric Boswell who later became part of the Ashford & Tenterden Aircraft Recovery Team – an organisation which subsequently went on to form the Brenzett Aeronautical Museum on Romney Marsh and not many miles distant from the Appledore crash site. However, it must be stressed that the present membership or organisation of that museum had *no* involvement or connection whatsoever with the excavations of the early 1970s. Further, the membership of Brenzett Museum (post the first dig on the Helmut Strobl crash site) and who recovered the aircraft of Werner Knittel and Richard Riedel were not involved, either. Indeed, the actions of David Buchanan and the team that worked with him at that time must be considered as beyond reproach. Considering what had clearly gone on here it would be fair to say that the coroner's comments were perhaps somewhat restrained. What is certain is that some local newspapers who had labelled such recoveries then being undertaken as by 'The Grave Robbers of Kent' did so with some justification. It was, perhaps, something that would continue to taint much future work of this kind and to colour the judgement of both the press and the public for a very long time into the future. That this should have partly eclipsed the otherwise good and valuable work that was going on is doubly unfortunate.

Lt Helmut Strobl (right) poses with other pilots of JG 27 on the Channel coast during the summer of 1940. On the left is Oblt Düllberg with Oblt Daig in the centre. It was Erwin Daig's duty to write to the Strobl family.

With the inquest formalities out of the way, and in a departure from the usual convention that had seen those Luftwaffe casualties discovered in post-war Britain being buried at Cannock Chase German Military Cemetery, Helmut Strobl was repatriated to his native Austria for burial in the hometown of his family, Kolbnitz. In a symbolic gesture he was laid to rest in the family plot on 5 September 1987 in an impressive ceremony attended by family members, former Luftwaffe fighter pilots, representatives of the Austrian armed forces, officials from the Austrian and German governments, civic dignitaries and also by Wg Cdr David McCann OBE on behalf of the RAF. At last, Helmut Strobl was at rest although it was clearly a ceremony that could and should have been performed some fifteen years earlier had those then involved acted appropriately and responsibly.

Author's Note: Andrew Cresswell continued to be actively involved in researching the background to various Battle of Britain incidents right up until November 2008 when he was tragically murdered after disturbing a burglary at his business premises.

CHAPTER 7 Fate Unknown?

WHILST THE LOSSES DEALT with in the previous chapters have virtually been open and shut cases, there are also those where tangible proof from either documentary or physical evidence exists to show what happened to a specific Luftwaffe airman or to complete or partial crews but, notwithstanding this, these casualties continue to be listed as missing. In such cases, either the evidence of bodily remains was non-existent at post-war excavations, or else no clue exists as to what became of personnel who were confirmed dead at the time but for whom no grave, whether named or unknown, has ever been traced. A case in point, and where documentary evidence exists to prove the pilot's death, was the crash of a Messerschmitt 109 E at Balmer Down, Sussex, almost exactly mid-way between Lewes and Brighton, on 1 October 1940.

Perhaps, and so as to ring the changes, we should look instead at a contemporary newspaper report of the period in respect of this incident rather than just the more formal and sterile official reports. In its article on 5 October 1940 the *Brighton and Hove Gazette* carried a small piece under the heading 'Battle over Brighton: Nazi Plane crashes on Farm'.

> The piece went on:
>
> "People in Brighton heard a battle above the clouds on Tuesday as British fighters went into action against a force of enemy raiders. Very little was seen of the fight (writes a *Gazette* reporter) until a Messerschmitt 109 power-dived through the clouds and crashed on a farm on the northern outskirts of the town. The Nazi pilot had been killed in mid air and his body was found in the wreckage of his plane which was smashed to pieces as it hit the ground at a terrific speed."

So, here in a contemporary report we have an account of the pilot having been killed and yet absolutely no trace exists locally of any burial that might be linked to this man. In confirmation of his death we do have the report of PC 118 John Bridger, in which he describes how "...both pilot and the machine were smashed to pieces". Further, he goes on to describe finding an identity disc bearing the number 60018/15. Here we have official confirmation of the discovery of the pilot's body, or at least some sight of the remains

This was the awful aftermath when a Messerschmitt 109 exploded on the chalk of the South Downs near Falmer, East Sussex. Both aircraft and occupant were smashed to pieces, and although the identity disc belonging to the pilot was found with the wreckage he has no known grave.

thereof, and the means by which to identify him. And yet, despite all this, there is absolutely no trace of this man being buried anywhere locally. Certainly, he is not buried under his name and it is possible to confirm from the identity disc number that this was thirty-year-old Uffz Johann Bluder of 4./JG 26. Bluder simply has no known grave, and neither is there any grave in the locality for an unknown airman that might possibly be linked to Hans Bluder.

Only one conclusion can be reached; the remains were simply not formally buried. Quite why this may be so is unclear, but the possibility exists that it was simply because insufficient weight was found to constitute a body and a convention seems to exist, or to have once existed, whereby a weight of seven pounds must be reached before a burial can take place. Either way, the German War Graves Service were able to confirm in August 1976 that they were aware that Johann Bluder had died at Brighton although noted: "Grave place not known".

If the theory about the weight of remains found is correct, then it would possibly explain the 'disappearance' of a number of Luftwaffe airmen. However, to all intents and purposes the rolling South Downs at Balmer Farm are the last resting place for Uffz Bluder who had most likely been shot down in a brief engagement with Spitfires of 41 Squadron. The case of Bluder, however, is not unique amongst Luftwaffe casualties over the British Isles, although it is one where we have indisputable documentary evidence of positive identification and the fact that bodily remains were certainly found. There are other equally intriguing cases, and ones where physical evidence of identification has since been discovered in excavations but no trace of the airmen could be found. One such is another Messerschmitt 110 shot down over Dorset.

Villagers at the tiny hamlet of Buckland Ripers, just to the north of Weymouth, were only just becoming used to the sights and sounds of the Battle of Britain when, on 25 August, the horror of that battle came right into their midst. Literally. At 17.30 hours Captain Norman Buckley, ARP warden at Buckland Ripers, telephoned Weymouth control to confirm that a German aeroplane with two engines and twin rudders had crashed into a field at Mr Symonds's farm after being shot down by aircraft. The report went on to state that the aircraft had sunk into the ground on contact, exploded and caught fire with the explosion flinging fragments of the aircraft and occupants for a distance of seventy yards. It was thought that one man had been trapped in the wreckage and the other had been blown out by the explosion since one partly burnt parachute was found in the field. Unlike the Long Bredy incident where most of the aircraft had buried itself deep in the soil leaving little to see on the surface, the scene in Moon Leas field was rather different and a crater blasted by the impact gave the impression that a bomb had exploded.

Certainly, wreckage of the plane and evidence of its unfortunate occupants had been scattered in and around the crater and despite the grisly scene the villagers turned out en masse to gawp and to gape but the scattered debris and scrap metal provided rich pickings for a gypsy family encamped in the adjacent wood. Rich pickings, that is, until a still gloved but mutilated hand so alarmed one of the women that the Romanies fled the scene. Not so deterred, however, was villager Margaret Ward who spied a sheet of grey leather from one of the fuel tank coverings. Grabbing her chance, Margaret knew that this would make a useful tea-pot mat. Such lack of concern for the occupants of the aircraft was perhaps typical of the time. The acquisition of some new trophy transcended any thought or concern for the two men who had just been blasted to eternity on this very spot just moments beforehand. More than thirty years later and Mrs Ward's tea-pot mat was still in use. Equally tangible were the vivid memories of the event still retained by local residents.

All of them were clear about one thing though, and that was that there really was very little left of the occupants and aside from one or two unpleasant finds the most significant manifestation of the two dead crew members had been the single burnt parachute. They were also clear that what could be seen of the aircraft in the crater was hauled out, whilst other bits of debris were heaved back into the hole before it was levelled over. As for the crew, well... that was left to nature.

In August 1981 village recollections of the event were re-awakened when an excavating team visited the site at Tatton House Farm to carry out an investigative dig. It would be an exercise where rather more than just local memories would be stirred up. On the 12th of that month the author joined Peter Foote, Steve Vizard, Steve Hall, John Ellis, Guy Smith, Simon Parry, Terry Parsons and William Hamblen (all of them experienced aviation archaeologists) to excavate fully the site in an attempt to discover not only what was there

One of the items unearthed during the August 1981 excavation of the crashed Messerschmitt 110 at Buckland Ripers, Dorset, was a complete parachute which billowed into the wind as it was discovered.

but who the crew had been. Apart from the date of the loss, very little else was known other than that it had been a Messerschmitt 110. However, on the date in question four Me 110 crews were still unaccounted for and the Buckland Ripers crash could be any one of those four. Might an excavation prove their identity and result in final burial for the two men? In the event, only one of those two hoped-for outcomes would be achieved.

Almost at once the mechanical excavator began to unearth evidence of the crash; heat exploded 7.92mm bullets, cannon shells, airframe fragments and bits of shattered Perspex. Then, something else. A greyish bundle emerged into the bright sunshine, and then out of this amorphous shape billowed a tattered but relatively intact parachute canopy – sure evidence that indeed both men had died here given the discovery of another parachute in 1940. Baulks of timber left behind by those who had pulled things out of the pit at the time were also intermingled with other discarded debris, including the rusted shell of a bucket. Inside were the remains of a hessian sack and underneath the sack a single leather glove. Had this been the glove that had so frightened the gypsy woman? Certainly, the parachute and the glove find were eerie echoes of identical discoveries in 1940.

Finally, fifteen feet apart and at about ten feet deep were both propeller hubs – proof that both engines and the bulk of whatever else might have been there had been recovered already in 1940. Quite probably any clues that might help identify the crew had been lost then, too. That said, examination of the propeller hubs showed the alloy spinner cones

Prior to the crash site excavation the identity of the aircraft and its two crew had been unknown, although this particular discovery revealed the Werke Nummer of the Messerschmitt 110 to be 3532. Unfortunately, the aircraft numbers of the various machines lost that day were not recorded and therefore this discovery did not help provide answers that might identify the crew.

impacted and compressed into their fronts by the terrific force of the crash – and each one had clearly been painted with a bright red tip. This colour was almost sufficient identification alone, since it was the correct colour for an 8 Staffel machine from whichever unit had been involved here. On checking the records only one aircraft really fitted the bill; a Messerschmitt 110 of 8./ZG 26 crewed by Fw Manfred Dähne and Obgefr Fritz Müller. However, rather more than just a few chips of red paint were needed to confirm an identity. What had been discovered thus far was only an indicator. It wasn't conclusive evidence by a long way.

With only a small pile of apparently insignificant wreckage to sift through it certainly seemed that the prospect of solving the mystery of this missing crew would elude the investigators. However, the discovery of a piece of cloth or canvas that had been clearly inscribed with the aircraft Werke Nummer (works number) bearing

This discovery, however, did provide the answers that were being sought. Engraved with the initials M D, the cigarette case can only have belonged to one pilot since amongst those Me 110 crewmen lost on 25 August 1940 these initials gave the only match.

the inscription W.Nr. 3532 initially gave some fresh hope. This was clearly the number of the aircraft but aside from confirming this to be a Messerschmitt Bf 110 C-4 series, it helped little further in identifying the crew. Unfortunately, at this stage of the war the Luftwaffe did not usually record the number of individual aircraft – leastways, they were not tied to specific crews. So, all that this discovery had achieved was to tell the investigators the hitherto un-recorded Werke Nummer of this particular Messerschmitt 110. Nothing more.

However, further sifting of the wreckage and spoil heap revealed more evidence of the two crew, first in the form of a mangled sole from a Luftwaffe flying boot and, more significantly, a badly damaged cigarette case. When the case was carefully cleaned it was found to be inscribed with the initials M D. Here at last was a clue to work with, and a quick check of the records revealed that only one crew lost that day had anyone on board with the initials M D. That was indeed the previously identified 8./ZG 26 crew with its pilot **M**anfred **D**ähne.

Nevertheless, and whilst the mystery had now been satisfactorily resolved for the investigators, the status of the crew remained classified as missing since no tangible trace of them had come to light during the excavations. Both men had, to all intents and purposes, completely disappeared with the awful forces of impact, fire and explosion – forces that had caused the terrible scenes witnessed at the crash site in 1940. However, whilst the men themselves had been lost without trace they had, at least, left behind one little clue that had enabled their very post-dated identification. With that clue the author made significant efforts during the 1980s to find relatives of the two men at least to let them know what had happened. Unfortunately, attempts to find either family eventually failed but maybe, one day, somebody will read these words and a connection will at last be made, thus enabling a line finally to be drawn under events more than seventy years on. Whether there might have been sufficient remains for the authorities to have buried in 1940 as two unknown airmen it is now impossible to say, but what happened then must have been very similar to the aftermath of the crash of Bluder's Messerschmitt 109 at Balmer Down. Clearly, whatever had been found at that time was either ignored or quietly disposed of, leaving absolutely no hope of these two men being named on their headstones by any evidence that might emerge long after the event. Given the clear evidence discovered in 1981 there can be little doubt that this information would have been more than sufficient for the German authorities to pronounce identification.

If evidence of identification from the Messerschmitt 110 loss at Buckland Ripers was firm and conclusive, then that recovered from another aircraft of the same type that had been downed in Hampshire at Slackstead Farm, Hursley, on 15 August 1940 was surely rather more tenuous. Again, the finds were the result of an excavation, this time led by Battle of Britain researcher Ian Hutton during July 1993 and carried out under a licence granted by the Ministry of Defence. Unlike the Buckland Ripers dig, which occurred before the licensing requirements of the Protection of Military Remains Act 1986 and thus did not require any official sanction, the Hursley site did. As with Buckland Ripers, the crew of this aircraft were unknown and missing and ordinarily this would have mitigated against the MOD granting a recovery licence although fortunately for Ian Hutton it could be shown that, whilst officially missing, both men had been recovered and buried in the local churchyard as unknown German airmen.

Although the remains had subsequently been transferred to Cannock Chase German Military Cemetery, still as unknowns, their prior removal from the crash site in 1940 had cleared the way for an excavation. The hope was that something could be found at the site positively to identify the crew and thereby enable two more missing men to be formally identified and named. After all, the earlier discovery at Buckland Ripers would have enabled those two crewmen to have been named had they already had a grave. There was no reason to suppose that something along the lines of the Buckland Ripers cigarette case find could not be found at Slackstead. All of the evidence certainly pointed to the engines and significant parts of the fuselage wreckage being still buried there, and Mr Phillips of Slackstead Manor Farm and Mr Randall of Upper Slackstead Farm were both adamant that little had ever been recovered. Clear, too, was former soldier Aubrey Rose:

In 1940 the remains of the two crew members were buried in nearby Hursley churchyard as unknown German airmen. They were exhumed during the 1960s and moved to Cannock Chase German Military Cemetery, still as unknown. Unfortunately, the 1993 excavations at the crash site failed to reveal any clues that might positively identify them.

> "I was a lance-corporal Skill at Arms & Drill Instructor with the King's Royal Rifle Corps at Bushfield Camp, Winchester, during the Battle of Britain and we often used to watch the dogfights over the fields of Hampshire as the Germans flew inland from the coast to bomb targets in the area of Winchester. Only on one occasion did a German bomber drop a stick of five bombs right across Bushfield Camp where I was based. The bombs were mostly ineffective but one hit some of the wooden spider huts we used as accommodation and caused some casualties which I had to help dig out. I can still recall seeing German aircraft being chased by RAF fighters which were blazing away with their machine guns. The Germans just carried on flying without seeming to be affected by the fighters' fire. I don't ever remember seeing one crash, but once when I was on guard duty at Bushfield we were taken by truck to guard the site of a downed German plane.

"It was about five miles away from camp and when we arrived we were greeted by what remained of the aircraft which had obviously exploded as there were bits of it strewn all over the place. There was not much left of the crew, just bits of uniform and body parts lying around the place. The field was ploughed and as I wandered on my beat around the crash I came across a piece of uniform in one of the furrows. On picking it up I found that there was an Iron Cross pinned to the piece of cloth. The Iron Cross had obviously been damaged in the intense heat of an explosion and it was quite badly buckled. I removed the piece of uniform and threw it away, something which I have regretted ever since, and pocketed the Iron Cross. I didn't tell my superiors about it as I was worried I would have to hand it in. I have always wondered who the medal had belonged to."

Lance Corporal Rose of the King's Royal Rifle Corps photographed in 1940 at around the time of the Slackstead Farm Messerschmitt 110 incident.

Seventy years later and Aubrey Rose returned to the crash scene. Here, he indicates the spot where he picked up this war trophy in 1940 – an Iron Cross First Class.

Ian Hutton led this excavation at the Slackstead crash site during July 1993. Unfortunately, no clues emerged to identify positively the crew involved in the loss of this aircraft. One of the recovered engines is now displayed at the Solent Sky Museum, Southampton.

Ian Hutton and his team wondered too, and also hoped they would be able to name its previous owner and to solve yet another little mystery from the Battle of Britain. Unfortunately, and despite a thorough excavation of the site down to a depth of around twelve feet, nothing could be found in the recovered wreckage to provide any *positive* identification, although there were a few tantalising clues. Ian Hutton explains:

"Several interesting items were recovered, including two engines, propeller bosses, the remains of a cannon and one undercarriage leg. There were also several other bits and pieces. Alas, the wreckage had obviously burnt furiously following the impact and consequently the data plates from the engines had all burnt away. Likewise, the markings on the gun barrel were unrecognisable and no numbers were found on any of the remaining fuselage structures. I had hoped that the cockpit area itself might have remained relatively unscathed, perhaps yielding some useful information; again, this area was reduced to ash, molten alloy and corroded aluminium oxide and so no papers, effects or suchlike were found.

"There was, however, one item in particular that was extremely interesting. This was a portion of thin steel plate that we were able to identify as part of one of the cannon firing troughs from under the front of the aircraft nose. Of itself, this was not a particularly significant or surprising find but the discovery that this was painted bright red was what interested us. Of the aircraft lost that day, some were from the unit ZG 76 and

„De Vliegende Haai" 2-motorige Messerschmidt Jager.

Portions of red paint from around the cannon ports were discovered during the dig. This clue pointed very strongly to the aircraft being a machine of one particular unit with the distinctive red shark's mouth emblem worn by that unit. This discovery helped narrow down the possible crews involved but was not in any way conclusive. This striking artwork is shown here on an aircraft of the same unit.

> their aeroplanes carried very distinctive sharks-mouth insignia on the nose. This comprised a large open red mouth bordered by white teeth, the whole emblem taking up the entire form of the fuselage in a fearsome display! The position of the gun trough would have been in the centre of the shark mouth, hence the red paint. So, at least we know the unit the aeroplane operated with."

In fact, and although the paint certainly indicated ZG 76, it did not necessarily assist in taking forward the identification to any positive conclusion. Indeed, what we had was confirmation that this aeroplane was actually from II Gruppe of ZG 76 (eg, either 4,5 or 6 Staffel) since it was only that group within ZG 76 that carried the sharks-mouth markings. So, drawing from the losses suffered by II./ZG 76 that day we have only two real contenders where there were missing crews; one from 5 Staffel and one from 6 Staffel. However, the further discovery of yellow paint on the tip of a spinner (in much the same way as the Buckland Ripers discovery) would point to the aeroplane of 6./ZG 76 being involved at the Slackstead crash. At this point, and at risk of losing the reader not familiar with the minutiae of Luftwaffe colour codings and tactical markings, the Staffel colours for II Gruppe were as follows: 4 Staffel – white, 5 Staffel – red, 6 Staffel – yellow. So, *prima facie*, this looks to be the 6 Staffel aeroplane. But is it?

Whilst we do not know the identity of the two German fliers it is possible to confirm their most likely attackers as Fg Off R A 'Butch' Barton and Plt Off J R B Meaker of 249 Squadron. Here, Barton poses with the squadron's pet duck 'Wilfred'. See his combat report on page 84.

Just to confound matters, another discovery that threw some doubt on the 6 Staffel identification was an ammunition clip from a small pistol. Almost certainly this was from a Walther Model 9, a side arm carried almost exclusively by officers. The problem with this discovery is that it points away from the 6./ZG 76 aeroplane which had a crew who were both NCOs. On the other hand, the other II Gruppe aeroplane with a missing crew was from 5./ZG 76 and this *did* have an officer on board, its pilot Oblt Gerhard Bremer. However, if it was his aeroplane then we should be expecting to see a red-tipped spinner for the 5th Staffel. Instead, we have the contra-indicator of the yellow-tipped spinner. On the balance of probability though, and notwithstanding the yellow paint, it does seem that the Slackstead crash *probably* involved Oblt Bremer and his gunner, Uffz Leo Pauli. Despite the apparent yellow spinner tip it could well have been that aeroplanes had been swapped around within II Gruppe to cover unserviceable machines for example. Either that, or it could have been a spare 'cannibalised' from another Me 110 or maybe some other unknown personal or tactical marking.

One could hypothesise endlessly. Perhaps in this case the jury is still out, although what is certain is that the evidence gleaned would most certainly be insufficient to convince the German authorities as to the identity of the two unknown airmen now resting at Cannock Chase. All in all it was a frustrating outcome for Ian Hutton and his team. Whilst the Slackstead crew remain missing and unidentified this case illustrates well the detailed and forensic examination of every existing clue and the interpretation of whatever evidence there is available.

Of course, the cases of the Messerschmitt 109 at Balmer Down and the Messerschmitt 110s at Buckland Ripers and Slackstead are just illustrative examples of many such instances where either the disappearance of aircrew or a complete inability to identify them had occurred. There were certainly many more. For example, it is known that the Kent Battle of Britain Museum (now based at Hawkinge) excavated prior to September 1971 the crash site of a Junkers 88 of 8./KG 77 at Mocketts Farm, Harty, on the Isle of Sheppey. It had crashed there on 18 September 1940 and resulted in the disappearance of two of its crew; Ofw

Semerau and Uffz Treutmann. Amongst the items recovered and subsequently displayed in the museum is an identity disc marked 65108/51 which can be tied to Treutmann although there are no reports of remains being discovered.

A similar case is that of another Messerschmitt 110 shot down on 11 September 1940. Again an excavation by the Kent Battle of Britain Museum, and again a case where an identity disc (marked 60043/21) was recovered. This number can be tied to Gefr Paul Eckert who continues to be listed as missing. Amongst the other artefacts recovered from the site during the dig were parachute buckles, a crewman's pistol and a cigarette case. Later, and after the excavation had been reinstated, a German wound badge was found laying on the surface of the field. They are finds which tell their own story.

Whether the relatives of Treutmann or Eckert are aware that evidence pointing to the disappearance of their kinsfolk has been on public display is unclear. However, when interviewed for *The Sunday People* in an article published on 28 October 1973 (at least two years after the Mocketts Farm Junkers 88 recovery) the museum's curator, Michael Llewellyn, is quoted as saying: "The only personal effects we have in our museum are those donated by pilot's relatives," and went on to add: "If we discovered a pilot's remains we would quit the site immediately and leave the wreckage where it is." Unfortunately, it has not been possible to verify or photograph the artefacts referred to above because of the museum's very strict ban on photography or any other form of recording including the use of notebooks as mentioned in a previous chapter.

There are other cases, too, where disappeared aircrew have left behind a puzzle that seems as though it should have been solved long ago. In that context we need look no further than the Messerschmitt 109 that crashed into Squirrel's Wood at Stockbury, Kent, on 18 September 1940 taking its pilot with it. When the site was excavated by the London Air Museum during the 1970s they found coins, a watch, maps, a parachute release box and the control column top but did not report finding any other trace of the pilot. Much later, Steve Vizard discovered the main aircraft constructor's plate stamped 5388 at the site, tying this aeroplane conclusively to Oblt R Krafftschick of 1./JG 27 who is yet another of the Luftwaffe missing from the Battle of Britain. However, the mystery was perhaps explained in more recent years when the elderly owner of the woodland confirmed that he had excavated there long before anyone else had touched the site, probably during the very early 1960s, and had found the body of the pilot. Perturbed by his discovery he filled in the hole and abandoned his diggings. Seemingly this is a case where post-war events have almost certainly resulted in a set of circumstances where this missing pilot will never be found, although all subsequent discoveries at the site have indicated that positive identification and formal closure of another case would have been a relatively simple matter had things been done properly.

As for our Slackstead Farm incident, Aubrey Rose has often pondered over who it was that once wore the Iron Cross First Class which he had picked up at the crash site. Was it Gerhard Bremer? Or was it someone else? Maybe, just maybe, that otherwise anonymous Iron Cross could yet be the clue that might unlock the identity of these two men? Perhaps if it were ever possible to find the families of all likely missing Messerschmitt 110 crews lost

COMBAT REPORT

FORM "F"

Sector Serial No. ....(A) ....

Serial No. of Order detailing Flight or Squadron to patrol ....(B) ....

Date ....(C) ..... 15.8.40.

Flight, Squadron ....(D) Flight ... B ...... Sqdn... 249.

Number of Enemy Aircraft ....(E) ..... 30-50.

Type of Enemy Aircraft ....(F) ... Bombers and ME.110.

Time Attack was delivered ....(G) .... 17.35.

Place Attack was delivered ....(H) .... Ringwood Area.

Height of Enemy ....(J) ..... 15,000 ft.

Enemy Casualties ....(K) ..... 1 ME.110 Destroyed 1 ME.110 Damaged.

Our Casualties, Aircraft ....(L) ..... Nil

Personnel ....(M) ..... Nil

Searchlights ....(N) ..... N/A

A.A. ....(P) ..... N/A

Range at which fire was opened and estimated length of burst ....(R) ....

GENERAL REPORT ....(S) .... See text. ....

... ordered to patrol Ringwood Area. Whilst leading Blue Section ... 50 enemy aircraft and ordered No.1 attack on rearmost section. ... turned and attacked Blue Section. ... Fired 2 sec. burst 30° deflection at ... 110 and observed smoke from engine, then attacked another 110 and fired ... bursts with full deflection (200 per hour deflection allowed). Saw my ... lets entering fuselage behind pilot, smoke poured from starboard engine. I followed enemy aircraft down and it crashed about four miles North West of Romsey. ... Rounds fired - 800.

Signature, R H Barton

(Section, Blue (F/Lt BARTON)

COMBAT REPORT 112/22

ector Serial No.....................(A)........Y 69..............

erial No. of Order detailing Flight or
quadron to patrol...................(B).............................

ate.................................(C)..15.8.40.....................

light, Squadron.....................(D)Flight..B......Sqdn...249....

umber of Enemy Aircraft.............(E)......30 - 50.................

ype of Enemy Aircraft...............(F)......Bombers and ME.110.

ime Attack was delivered............(G)......17.35...................

Place Attack was delivered..........(H)......Ringwood Area.

Height of Enemy.....................(J)......15,000 ft.

Enemy Casualties....................(K)......1 ME.110 Destroyed.

Our Casualties, Aircraft............(L)......Nil

Personnel...........................(M)......Nil

Searchlights........................(N)......N/A

A.A.................................(N2).....N/A

Range at which fire was opened and estimated
length of burst.....................(P)....See text.

GENERAL REPORT......................(R)..I was Blue 2 and followed
e Leader (F/Lt Barton) in No. 1 attack, but got into a spin. On coming
of spin saw four ME.110 circling and picked out one giving full deflec-
n ~~xxxx~~ burst on beam. He took violent evasive action, but I gave him
ther bursts and saw streams of white vapour from both engines. I fol-
ed him to 500 ft. and saw him crash about 10 miles North of Southampton.
nds fired - 2,400.

Signature, JRB Meaker P/O
(P/O J.R.B. MEAKER)

Plt Off J R B Meaker, who also engaged Messerschmitt 110s over Hampshire on 15 August in the action when the Slackstead aircraft was brought down. Meaker was killed in action on 27 September 1940.

These personal effects recovered from the crash site of a Messerschmitt 109 in Squirrel's Wood, Stockbury, Kent, tell their own story. Sadly, their former owner, Oblt Krafftschick, is still missing with no known grave despite an excavation at the crash site during the very early 1960s by the landowner. During that excavation human remains are said to have been disturbed. A subsequent excavation of the site by the London Air Museum in the 1970s revealed these items.

that day then identification might be possible by a process of elimination? If, perchance, only one of those four crewmen happened to be the recipient of an Iron Cross First Class then that could be the vital clue. It is certainly what one might fairly call a long shot, but there again those involved in investigations of this kind would never say never!

CHAPTER 8

Down on The Farm

THE TEN-DAY PERIOD from 8 August 1940 had seen some of the hardest fighting thus far in the Battle of Britain, with German air attacks against airfield targets reaching their peak on 18 August – now recognised by historians as the hardest fought day of the entire battle. Immediately after the supreme effort that took place on that day it was almost as if the Luftwaffe was pausing to catch its breath and for the period between 19 and 23 August German air operations against the British Isles were comparatively few in number and low-key in tempo, although that in part was surely due to deteriorating weather conditions. Contrary to popular belief, the summer of 1940 was not always the blazingly glorious weather that legend now tends to suggest. However, and whatever the weather, elements of I and II Gruppen of KG 54 were detailed on 21 August for raids against British targets; the airfields at Brize Norton and Abingdon and the Supermarine Spitfire factory at Southampton. They would turn out to be costly operations for KG 54.

The first attack of the day involved a I Gruppe machine from the 1st Staffel which departed during the late morning from its base at Evreux, France, headed for an attack against the Supermarine works at Eastleigh although its course and the run-in to target had taken it in a circuitous route from St Alban's Head and then inland to Shaftesbury where the bomber swung west towards Salisbury. At the controls, twenty-two-year-old Ogefr. Gerhard Freude adjusted his course as Salisbury slipped past underneath and he now headed down south east towards the next way-mark at Romsey. The target at Eastleigh was just a few miles beyond Romsey, and after striking it on a run-in from the north west the bomber would then take a steep turn to port before heading back on itself and then out over the New Forest to depart the English coast between The Needles and Bournemouth. That, at least, was the plan.

Alerted to the presence of the lone bomber, the Y Sector controller in 10 Group RAF Fighter Command, Flt Lt Paul Richey, sent off Red Section (three aircraft) of 234 Squadron Spitfires from Middle Wallop at 13.20 to intercept and guided the trio through the poor weather until they eventually spotted the bomber just after Freude had made his course adjustment over Salisbury. The Spitfires, flown by 234 Squadron's new CO, Sqn Ldr J S O'Brien (Red 1), Flt Lt C L Page (Red 2) and Plt Off R F T Doe (Red 3), moved in for the kill and O'Brien and Doe raked the Junkers 88 with fire and closing in to between thirty and

Lfd. Nr.	Ort und Tag des Verlustes, Feindflug? ja oder nein?	Staffel usw.	Dienstgrad, Dienststellung	Vorname	Familienname, Truppenteil, Nr. der Erkennungsmarke	Geburts- tag	ort	kreis	Gefallen*)	Verwundet **) Körperstelle und Waffe *) schwer	leicht	Vermißt gefangen	sonstig
1	2	3	4	5	6	7	8	9	10	11	12	13	14
1.	Feindflug auf Quaianlagen von Nieuport 27.5.1940.	2.	Ofw.	Hans	H e u ß n e r I./K.G.54, 2.St. 60 025/12	[redacted]	[redacted]	[redacted]					
2.	Feindflug Evreux-St. Alban's Head-Shaftesbury-Salisbury-Romsay-Eastleigh - Linkskurve, Ausflug: englische Südküste zwischen Bournemouth und The Needles. 21.8.1940.	1.	Ogefr. Flgzgf.	Gerhard	F r e u d e I./K.G. 54, 1.St. 60 024/67	14. 10. 18	Koslitz	Lüben	Weiterer Verbleib ist				+
3.	"	1.	Oblt. Bomben-schütze	Max-Dankwart	Birkenstock I./K.G. 54, 1.St. 60 024/4	16. 12. 15	Neu-stettin	Stettin Brenneke	Gerichtlich für tot				+
4.	"	1.	Uffz. Bordfk.	Rudolf	S c h u l z e I./K.G.54, 1.St. 60 024/64	29. 9. 19	Liegnitz	Liegnitz	"	"		"	+
5.	"	1.	Gefr. Bordschütze	Franz	B e c k e r I./K.G. 54, 1.St. 60 024/79	18. 1. 19	Hürth	Köln	Weiterer Verbleib ist				+

+ für Lfd. Nr. 3 Kameraden ausschaffen. 10.9.58

Hauptmann und

*) Abkürzungen: K. = Kopf, H. = Hals, Br. = Brust, Ba. = Bauch, R. = Rücken, l. A. = linker Arm, (J. G. = Infanterie-Geschoß, H. Gr. = L. = Luftkampf, A. = Absturz)

**) Hierzu rechnen auch Verstauchungen und Verrenkungen durch stumpfe Gewalt infolge feindlicher Einwirkung, durch Verschüttung usw.

The losses of all Luftwaffe personnel detailed in this book were reported officially by the unit concerned to Berlin. This is the report document for the crew of the Junkers 88 brought down at King's Somborne on 21 August 1940.

fifty yards during their attacks. Initially, the gunner Gefr Franz Becker returned fire but eventually, noted the RAF pilots, all answering fire had ceased although not before Becker had put a bullet through Doe's wing. With the Junkers 88 crippled, the RAF pilots watched as the stricken enemy machine fell earthwards before crashing violently into open fields north of the Hampshire village of King's Somborne and just alongside the Stockbridge Road.

To an extent it had been an easy 'kill' for the Spitfire pilots and for Doe, having only first been in action just six days earlier, this was his fifth victory. This time, it was a shared claim

ßerhalb der ng infolge von		Abgegeben an welche Behörde des Feindes (Krankenhaus) und weshalb	Bemerkung: z. B. Grablage oder bei 17 vermutlich übergelaufen. Art und Stärke der feindlichen Waffenwirkung bzw. näh. Umstände. Letzter Wohnort des Toten.
Un-fall	Selbst-mord		
17	18	19	20
		[redacted] Res.-Lazarett II [redacted] Kassel-Neuemühle eingeliefert.	Maschine am 21.8.40. zum Feindflug gestartet und nicht zurückgekehrt.

kannt

56 Pr.

nt.

andeur.

gung, Gs. B.

with his CO, Sqn Ldr O'Brien, who had not previously shot down any enemy machines. Excited by the achievement, O'Brien was keen to go and have a look at the wreck and drove Bob Doe across from Middle Wallop to the crash scene which was a still smouldering pile of wreckage surrounding a blackened scar that had been slashed across a farmer's field.

Up until now, Doe had been insulated from the nastier realities of shooting down aeroplanes.

401

Offen versenden!

Absendende Dienststelle
Ersatztruppenteil mit Standort

I./Kampfgeschwader Nr. 54

Reichsluftfahrtministerium
Eing. -3 SEP.1940
Vorm.-Nachm.

Vordruck II

Namentliche Verlustmeldung

Nr. 23 *)

über

Offiziere, Wehrmachtbeamte, Unteroffiziere und Mannschaften

Berichtszeitraum 17.8. – 24.8.1940

Verteiler:

Auf dem Dienstwege an L. Wehr 2
unmittelbar an Gen. Qu. 6. Abt.
" " Wehrmachtauskunftstelle für Kriegsverluste und Kriegsgefangene, Berlin W 30, Hohenstaufenstr. 47/48
" " Chef L. P.
Gen.Kdo. V.Fl.-Korps auf dem Dienstwege
K.G. 54
z. d. A.

*) Von absendender Dienststelle mit der lfd. Nr. auszufüllen.

Kleimann-Druckerei, Münster

Flt Lt Paul Richey was an experienced fighter pilot who had learnt his craft flying 1 Squadron Hurricanes during the Battle of France. By the time of the Battle of Britain he was being 'rested' and acted as a fighter controller. On 21 August he controlled fighters from Middle Wallop in their interception of the Ju 88 brought down at King's Somborne.

They were just machines and he had had to have little thought for the men they contained. On arrival at the crash site he was assailed by the sight and the stench; burning rubber, fuel, oil, magnesium….and flesh. It was an awful smell, but worse was to come. Eagerly, an elderly home guardsman approached Doe, gleefully holding up a blood-soaked flying helmet. In it were five bullet holes. With his stomach churning, Doe couldn't get back to O'Brien's car quickly enough. He couldn't get out of his mind the sight or the smell, or the awful reality that he had just killed four men. On the drive down from Middle Wallop he had felt smugly pleased with himself. With his previous tally, this had taken him up to five confirmed claims – in other words, he had now reached 'ace' status. Suddenly, that achievement seemed to have had the gloss taken off it and he wished that he had not gone along. Seeing the results of his handiwork was not something he would ever wish to repeat.

After the RAF pilots had left the field of their victory, the locals continued to come and gawp. Young boys vied for the best souvenirs, whilst tales of the downing of the German aircraft were told and re-told by those who were there – doubtless gaining more than a little embellishment, and probably a little less credibility, with each telling. Really the story that has never been told though, or at least not adequately explained, is what happened to Gerhard Freude and Franz Becker along with their two fellow crewmen Max-Dankwart Birkenstock and Rudolf Schulze. Officially, no trace of any of them has ever been found.

Village policeman PC Charlie Wykes had his work cut out trying to hold back the crowds and attempting to keep order, and when he first arrived on the scene he was alarmed to see what appeared to be a scatter of bombs lying in the burning wreckage. Public safety was also an issue. Being ordered back to a safer distance, the growing crowd at first crouched behind a low bank some two hundred yards from the wreck until the nature of the worrying looking cylinders became apparent and they were identified as the on-board oxygen bottles. From then on, PC Wykes could do very little on his own to keep the crowds of people away. What little of the crop that had not been spoiled by the crash, or by splattered fuel and oil and burning debris, was now comprehensively trampled by curious

Plt Off R F T 'Bob' Doe, a Spitfire pilot with 234 Squadron, was one of the successful RAF pilots who had engaged the Junkers 88 on 21 August 1940.

visitors – official and unofficial. Farmer Morgan of Manor Farm, on whose land the aircraft had fallen, could do little either to keep people away. His eight-year-old daughter, Barbara Broadbridge (née Morgan) recalled the event vividly sixty years later:

> "My mother, my sister, a friend and myself were blackberrying when the German plane roared over our heads with a fighter plane in hot pursuit. It then passed low over the field where my father and brother were busy harvesting. My brother, who was seventeen, took a pot shot at it with his gun which he had with him in case he saw a rabbit. The plane came down in the next field and I can vividly remember the great plume of black smoke and the horrible smell. My father was one of the first on the scene. There were no survivors. For many years nothing would grow in that part of the field."

That the crew of this aircraft all perished there can be no doubting whatsoever, and there is ample evidence that there were no survivors just as Barbara Broadbridge had testified. Indeed, cub-reporter Derek J Tempero was just eighteen years old when the Junkers 88 crashed and he had arrived with the crowds of sightseers just after the crash to get his scoop. What Tempero clearly recalled were the mutilated bodies of the four German fliers being placed in the back of an army truck and driven out of the field. On this point he is adamant. Olive Moldon, another King's Somborne resident, recalled that the parish vicar also turned up in the field and made it clear that he wanted the men buried at the parish church. According to Olive, though, his parishoners objected strongly and the vicar was over-ruled in his intended act of Christian decency. So, if Derek Tempero and Olive Moldon are accurate in their recall then this begs the question; where *were* the four men buried?

The smouldering wreckage of the Junkers 88 in the field at King's Somborne on 21 August. On the left, a group of RAF officers seem to be departing the field. The group quite probably includes 'Bob' Doe.

There is, quite simply, no record of any burial for these four airmen, identified or otherwise, anywhere in the vicinity and widening the search out much further there is no possible corresponding burial (or burials) anywhere in the country. Not only that, but there are no unidentified airmen buried at the Cannock Chase German Military Cemetery with a corresponding date of death, either. From the moment the aircraft crashed into that Hampshire field, or at least from the point when an army truck possibly drove the bodies *out* of the field, Freude, Birkenstock, Schulze and Becker completely vanish. There are, though, intriguing postscripts to the tale of the King's Somborne Junkers 88, and at least one element certainly highlights the ferocity of local anti-Germanic feeling that pervaded until long after the war.

Quite what it was that led the secretary of the local branch of the British Legion to suggest in 1948 that a memorial cross be erected to the four unknown Germans in the parish churchyard is unclear. However, whispers and rumours of some kind of collective village guilt have persisted ever since August 1940. Was it this that led Charles Bowyer to put forward the idea of the memorial cross? If it was, then that supposed collective guilt, or any sense of community forgiveness and reconciliation, was apparently lost on the wider population of the village. It was not an idea that had any public support, and it was quietly dropped whilst arrangements were put in hand to remember the village's own war dead on the local war memorial. Within a couple of years, however, the matter had come to the surface again when the parish council received three letters from Germany during

Franz Becker (left) poses with his best friend Karl Wenz. Through sickness, Wenz was not flying on 21 August 1940 although he ordinarily made up part of that crew. Karl failed to return from a flight over the Atlantic later in the war.

September 1950 (sic) asking about the airmen. One was from the parents of an officer, asking about their son. If this is correct then the letter can only have come from the parents of Max-Dankwart Birkenstock who was the only officer on board the Ju 88, the others all being NCOs.

How or why the Birkenstock family had settled upon the village of King's Somborne to address their query is unclear, but it is entirely possible they had established this was the only likely location in the British Isles where their son could have been killed since there were no other unaccounted-for enemy losses that day involving crashes on land. Whilst we do not know the nature of any reply that was sent back to Germany, it certainly seems likely that the Birkenstock family had at least deduced where their son had fallen. What they wanted to know, although nobody could tell them, is where he was buried. The evidence, unfortunately, seems to be that none of the four men were ever properly buried.

Following on from the queries out of Germany the question of a memorial again raised its head and on 30 October 1950 a parish meeting was called in the village school to discuss the matter when it was again proposed that a cross be erected in the cemetery. The level of interest engendered by this meeting can be gauged by the report of *The Romsey Advertiser* which told how "....the younger element of the village peered in at the windows as their elders crowded into the schoolroom." In fact, it was not only the parochial press who took an interest in proceedings and there were several reporters present from the national newspapers. Ultimately, the vote was defeated by twenty-eight votes to twenty-six against the memorial being sited in the village burial ground. But it was still not the end of the matter.

Mrs Flora Firbank of Hoplands Estate had pointed out at the meeting that the aircraft could have quite easily fallen in the village and she felt strongly that there should be a memorial – whatever the village vote. Consequently, she offered her land for the erection of a monument and it was decided to position it exactly below the final flight-path of the

The Junkers 88 crew were never buried and post-war controversy inflamed and polarised local opinion when the idea of a memorial to the four Germans was proposed. Ultimately, the village of King's Somborne rejected the idea of any commemoration. Instead, others who felt strongly about the matter had this simple monument erected some long distance away and just across the border into the next parish. The memorial bears an incorrect date (23 instead of 21 August) and is hidden away in a very remote location.

Junkers 88, albeit that this was some two miles from the crash site. By January 1951 parish records show that a memorial had been "procured" and by the spring of that year it had been dedicated in a small ceremony attended by some of the villagers whilst the others stayed away. Sensitive to public opinion, the memorial was in the form of a tablet rather than a cross – there being a view in some quarters that remembering these German airmen with a Christian symbol was 'inappropriate'.

By analysis of the losses suffered by the Luftwaffe that day it can certainly be concluded that the King's Somborne aircraft was that flown by Freude and his crew, and in 1989 the author established contact with Anni Weiss, the former fiancée of Franz Becker. Anni was able to tell how she and the Becker family were greatly relieved to know what had happened to him, writing:

> "Now, we know for sure that they didn't fall into the sea because that would have been very painful for him. He was one of the best swimmers in Germany at the time, and we had always worried that he had swum until exhausted and then drowned. Now we know it must have been over quickly, and we also know where he fell. We thank you for that comforting knowledge."

The tragedy of loss was compounded for the Becker family who had certainly endured their share of grief. One of twelve children, Franz was the first to die in the war although his parents had already suffered the pain of loss when three of his siblings had earlier died in infancy. After Franz, his brother was then killed at Stalingrad. Then, two other brothers became the victims of air raids. With them, two children of the eldest sister of Franz also died. One of them, her son, was in the navy and came home on leave the day before the air raid that took his life. Here was a family torn apart by war and it seems only appropriate that, because of this, he should be remembered at King's Somborne even if not by name. This book is also dedicated to his memory.

If Franz Becker had not died at sea in the harrowing way that his family had sometimes imagined, then the same could not be said for another KG 54 Junkers 88 crew also lost later on 21 August 1940. Lt Alfred Kiefer, Gefr German Plage, Gefr Hans Numberger and Flg Erwin Tilgner of the 4th Staffel (II Gruppe) were lost during a later attack that day, their aeroplane being shot down into the English Channel. Luckier were their colleagues from the same Staffel, Ofw Heinz Apollony, Hptm Lothar Maiwald, Uffz Kurt Miethner and Uff Helmut Hempel all being taken prisoner of war after a safe forced-landing at Earnley in West Sussex.

One mystery remains, however. In the German records *(Namentliche Verlustmeldung)* there is a margin note against the names of Birkenstock and Shultze, stating that both had subsequently been judicially declared dead. A tantalising note also refers to correspondence from comrades of Birkenstock on 10 September 1958. Could this in any way relate, perhaps, to the correspondence we know to have been received in the village during the 1950s? Although Birkenstock and Shultze seem to have been formally declared dead by some process or other, the same cannot be said for Freude and Becker. Against their names is recorded: "Further whereabouts not known".

Still shaken by his visit to the crash scene, Bob Doe flew his bullet-damaged Spitfire down to Eastleigh the following morning for repair and found himself being entertained to lunch by the work's foreman's wife. Hearing his tale, Doe's host exclaimed that she had watched that very engagement. Neither of them could have known that the Junkers 88 had as its target the Eastleigh site where her husband worked. Had it found its way to that target then the outcome could have been very different for all of them.

CHAPTER 9 Stuka Down!

THERE CAN BE NO doubting at all that one of the most famous photographs from the Battle of Britain is the image captured by a Thomson Newspaper Group photographer of a Junkers 87 Stuka diving to destruction above the rooftops of Chichester on 18 August 1940. It is reproduced in perhaps almost every book on the Battle of Britain; an iconic image of an iconic weapon. It is also one that hides the story behind another missing Luftwaffe airman from the Battle of Britain.

Post-war research has shown that 18 August was in fact the hardest fought day of the battle in terms of losses suffered by both sides and a considerable number of those sustained by the Luftwaffe on this day were Junkers 87 Stuka dive-bombers. In fact, it was the last outing of the Ju 87 Stuka in any significant numbers for the remainder of the 1940 air assaults against Great Britain. As for the photograph, its repeated use since 1940 led chartered surveyor and Battle of Britain researcher Ian Hutton to look into the detailed background of the incident. In fact, the event is almost as well recorded in written archives as it is photographically and the identity of the aircraft with its two crewmen is amply documented. What struck Ian, however, was the fact that one of the two men was listed as missing with no known grave and he resolved to do something about it if he could. When he discovered that the missing man was one of the many buried as an unknown German airman, his mission to do the right thing was focussed and single minded. To quote Ian: "If these pictures of his death were going to be published all the time I felt that we at least owed it to him to put a name on his grave."

In howling earthwards above the well-populated city of Chichester at around 14.30 hours on a sunny Sunday afternoon, it was inevitable that the stricken Stuka would be seen by hundreds of city dwellers. Many more would later trudge across the city and through fields near its outskirts to view the shattered wreckage which had exploded and burnt out on impact. What was left lay in a deep crater with its unexploded bombs. One of those who watched the battle, saw the German aircraft in its terminal dive and later went to view the scene was Leslie Holden, then twenty-five. What he saw he recorded in his diary:

> "Sunday 18 August. Between 2.15 and 3.25 pm (one of many warnings today) great activity. Saw two aircraft come down in a westerly direction and also a parachutist in the

Terminal dive. This dramatic picture depicts a Junkers 87 Stuka diving to destruction over Chichester, West Sussex. This amazing photograph of a powerful weapon of war hides the story of another hitherto 'missing' German flier.

same direction. Great deal of smoke in the direction of Thorney Island. A German aircraft crashed in the field immediately adjoining the children's home, bounded by St Paul's Road and opposite the junction of Parklands Road. Could see the smoke from my bedroom window at 104 Orchard Street. Went to the site after the all-clear sounded. Large crowd of people had gathered. I climbed the fence and entered the field. Saw the charred remains of the aircraft. Police arrived and turned people away.

Monday 19 August. Together with Sam Salter tried to view the aircraft. There is a 'No Thoroughfare' notice to Old Broyle Farm from Parklands as there are unexploded bombs in the aircraft. All children have been evacuated from the home."

Then, some days later, Leslie went there again, noting on 27 August that he had once more accompanied his friend Sam Salter and the pair had "had a good rummage amongst the

Impact! The blazing wreckage of the Junkers 87 Stuka in a field at The Broyle, Chichester, photographed shortly after it had crashed.

wreckage". Both of them salvaged trophies of their visit, Sam a part of the engine that would make a nice paperweight and Leslie a data plate marked Weser Flugzeugbau. Their curiosity still not satisfied the pair went back once more, this time on 29 August when they discovered that another unexploded bomb, and evidently the last, had been found since their last visit. (Caught on its run-in to the intended target of RAF Thorney Island the Stuka had not yet delivered its load, hence the discovery of bombs in the wreckage.) Although it was apparently their last visit to the site, the wreckage continued to attract sightseers for days if not weeks. Not only was this one of the most photographed Battle of Britain incidents but it must almost have been one of the most visited, too.

In fact, it was also visited by the Germans when, on 4 September 1940, the Luftwaffe carried out aerial photo reconnaissance of the district and unknowingly photographed the crash site from several thousand feet above. Clearly visible is the impact crater. Also clearly visible leading across the meadows of Broyle Farm to the crater from various access points into the field are well-trodden paths, newly stamped out by hundreds of feet. Despite all of this interest, however, there was very little concern for the pilot of the Stuka who lay for days mangled inside the wreckage.

Many of those who visited the scene have similar recollections of seeing a flying boot with its contents lying in the bottom of the crater. Ron Dynes ran to the site from his home in Walnut Avenue and picked up a Luger P08 pistol with a completely bent barrel as he crossed the field towards the crash. When he got there he peered into the smoking crater and saw the flying boot with a leg still in its flying suit trouser. Along with others he watched dispassionately as an undertaker arrived with a coffin and began placing the remains into it. This terrible sight, recalled by so many, is talked about in Chichester over seventy years later and is part of the lore and legend of this city's Battle of Britain experience. The dreadful scene that scores had witnessed first-hand was the ghastly aftermath of the young pilot's death, and although he had fared no better than his pilot the gunner had managed to get out of the dive bomber as it plummeted headlong into the ground. Unfortunately, he fell dead nearby with an unopened parachute and his crumpled body also attracted the morbidly curious to come and gape. Nonetheless, he and his unfortunate comrade were duly removed from the scene and afforded the usual Christian burial rites along with full military honours.

When they sifted through the crater, RAF intelligence officers retrieved a document showing the unit involved as StG 77 (in fact it had been 3./StG77) and initially at least there is documentary evidence to show that both crew members were identified by name; Uffz Erich Kohl and Uffz August Dann. Once this had happened, however, matters became somewhat muddled and for reasons that remain unknown the two airmen were separated when they were eventually taken away for burial. Logically, both men *should* have been buried within the Chichester administrative district but neither logic nor conformity, it seems, had been followed in this case. In the event, only one man was buried locally at Chichester Cemetery and although he was initially buried as unknown his name was later changed on the burial register to E Kohl. This man was the airman who had fallen from the Stuka before it crashed. For reasons that are unknown, however, the body that had been

American journalists, reporting on the Battle of Britain, are shown the crash site of the Stuka as they pick their way amongst the scattered fragments of wreckage.

extracted from the crater caused by the crashing aircraft had been taken away for burial at Portsdown Cemetery in Hampshire – many miles away from the place of his death and well outside the administrative boundaries of Chichester.

He was buried here as an unknown German airman on 21 August 1940 with his place of death recorded as Pitts Farm, The Broyle, Chichester. There can be no doubting that this man came from that Stuka crash, and given that the names of Kohl and Dann were recorded initially by the British authorities and it is known that Erich Kohl had been buried at Chichester it is simply a process of elimination which identifies the Portsdown burial as August Dann. Certainly, we know from German records that Dann and Kohl formed the crew of this particular Junkers 87.

In common with many German airmen buried around the British Isles, Erich Kohl and the unidentified airman from Portsdown Hill had been exhumed during the 1960s and re-buried at Cannock Chase German Military Cemetery. However, with the paper trail still extant a case for naming the unknown man formerly at Portsdown was presented by Ian Hutton to the German authorities during January 2001 and by 5 December that year the German War Graves Service had confirmed that the evidence presented by Ian had been accepted and that the grave of this hitherto unknown man at Cannock Chase would be marked with a headstone named to August Dann. (Author's Note: In cases such as these, and where evidence of identification is presented to the German War Graves Service, it is the German military archive in Berlin, the Deutsche Dienstelle (WASt), who are the final arbiter to confirm or refuse formal identification. This mirrors the position with British casualties vis-a-vis The Commonwealth War Graves Commission and the Ministry of Defence.)

All in all, this was a more than satisfactory outcome for Ian Hutton who had earlier been disappointed at being unable to offer definite identification for the two men killed in the

On 4 September 1940 the Luftwaffe carried out a photo-reconnaissance mission over the Chichester area and unknowingly captured on film the crash site of the Stuka which shows up as a white speck (circled) in the field off The Broyle. Radiating out from the crater are the well-trodden footpaths of scores of sightseers who flocked to the site for weeks after the event.

Slackstead Farm Messerschmitt 110. Knowing that the family of Dann were exceedingly grateful for all his work in having August named surely made his efforts worthwhile. The 'unknown' man linked to this world famous photograph now lies beneath a headstone that will be marked with his name – just as Ian intended when he embarked upon his mission to put matters right. However, and aside from his project with the Slackstead Farm Messerschmitt 110 crew, Ian also pursued some other cases of unknown German airmen where he felt there was evidence enough to name them.

On 14 August 1940 a Junkers 88 A-1 of 1./LG 1, shot down near North Charford was one of three which had taken part in a bombing attack against the airfield at RAF Middle Wallop, Hampshire, wreaking havoc when bombs hit the No.5 hangar. Blast tore the roof off the entire building and destroyed three Blenheims and several Spifires parked inside. As they struggled to close the heavy steel doors when the raid was approaching the airfield, three airmen were killed as the massive doors were literally blown off their rails on top of

Uffz August Dann, pilot of the Junkers 87 Stuka that plunged to destruction above the rooftops of Chichester on 18 August 1940.

them. As a result of the raid, three civilian contractors were also killed, with at least one other airman and fifteen civilians wounded. Although it had been a devastating event, retribution was swift.

Already airborne from Middle Wallop had been two Spitfires of 609 Squadron, flown by Fg Off John Dundas and Sgt Alan Feary. Seeing a twin-engined aircraft approaching from the south, Dundas and Feary moved in closer to investigate. After all, there were Blenheims operating from Middle Wallop with 604 Squadron and the pair needed to be sure this was not one of their machines on an air test. Sight of the German crosses was sufficient evidence and Dundas closed in for what was an inconclusive quick burst before it dived into cloud. Following it, Feary came out of cloud to find the aircraft (a Junkers 88) bombing the airfield and closed for the kill. From 250 yards Feary gave an astonishingly long burst of fire, loosing off no less than ten seconds worth of ammunition. The bomber was doomed almost at once, although Sgt Feary closed for the *coup-de-grâce*, finishing off what little ammunition he had left.

Out of control, the aircraft crashed in flames and disintegrated near Dead Mans Hill. Witness Jim Long recalled with horror the carnage at the scene, and the cries of an injured man for help. One man, Gefr E Sauer, had managed to escape by parachute and survived whilst the man recalled by Jim Long, Gefr F Ahrens, was captured badly wounded but died the next day in Salisbury Infirmary. The other two crew were still in the aircraft when it crashed and their terribly burned bodies defied all efforts to identify who they were. Consequently, they were buried in the Devizes Road Cemetery, Salisbury, as two unknown German airmen alongside their comrade Gefr Sauer. Despite the evidence that might have reasonably linked the three men by association, no formal connection was made by the German War Graves Service when the men were exhumed for re-burial at Cannock Chase. However, they can have been none other than the two unaccounted-for crewmen who had flown with Ahrens and Sauer and this was another case presented to the German authorities in 1999 by Ian and ultimately accepted. As a result, Oblt W Heinrici and Gefr H-W Stark are no longer missing.

If the cases of Dann, Heinrici and Stark were all relatively straightforward and without

Wreckage of the Junkers 88 at North Charford.

contention then another tackled by Ian Hutton was, perhaps, less so. Like the case of August Dann it involved a crash close to Chichester, also on 16 August, where it was reported that remains were found but where any grave location for the casualty was a mystery. This was the case of a Messerschmitt 110 shot down at Shopwyke House, right on the edge of the airfield at RAF Tangmere. Commonsense might well have suggested that any burial ought to have taken place in the war graves plot at St Andrew's Churchyard, Tangmere. The churchyard was literally within sight of the crash location and a number of Luftwaffe airmen were already buried there although there was no trace of any linking burial at St Andrew's. And neither was there any apparent trace of a burial that might be associated with this incident *anywhere* else in the district. In view of the case involving August Dann and his inexplicable burial at far-away Portsdown, Ian wondered if perhaps the man from Shopwyke House could have been taken there, too? And indeed, when he checked, it turned out there was another mystery burial at Portsdown and this, in his view, *could* have had a link. That said, there were immediately obstacles that stood in the way of making any connection with the man from Shopwyke although Ian Hutton was not to be deterred.

The Messerschmitt 110 shot down at Shopwyke House on 16 August 1940 was almost certainly a machine of II./ZG 76 flown by Lt Walter Lemmer with his crew member, Obgefr Josef Lewandowski. Last seen thirty kilometres north of Brighton, both men had been listed as missing although German records indicate that a signal that Lemmer was certainly dead was received on 8 August 1941. It is not clear by what means his death had been confirmed or why his colleague, Lewandowski, had apparently not been similarly listed as having *his*

On 16 August 1940 a Messerschmitt 110 was shot down above RAF Tangmere and crashed vertically into an ornamental pond at nearby Shopwyke House.

death confirmed. What is clear, though, is that a Messerschmitt 110 dived vertically into the grounds of Shopwyke House and hit an ornamental pond in the expansive gardens at approximately 17.39 hours that day and its crew died. Those who went to the site, including Police Sgt Cecil Morris, found the unpleasant spectacle of the torso of one of the crew hanging in an adjacent tree with the body still wearing its parachute harness. Morris had the unpleasant task of retrieving the German airman, although what became of the body from thereon is a mystery. Certainly, and in view of the nature of what was recovered, it would absolutely beggar belief that these remains were simply lost or disposed of. The question was; who was it and where were they buried? Easier to answer, although not helping to solve the mystery, was the question as to who had shot the aircraft down.

Writing to the author in December 1984, Wg Cdr Sir Archibald Hope Bt, described events that led to the destruction of the Messerschmitt. Then a Flt Lt (Acting Sqn Ldr), Hope was clear in his recall:

> "On that occasion I was flying my own Hurricane, UF-P, when we were instructed to patrol base at the relatively low altitude of 4,500 feet. This went on for a long time, rather over an hour, and I was leading twelve aircraft of 601 Squadron. Suddenly, when we were north east of the aerodrome (Tangmere) we saw an aircraft appear out of the cloud which I seem to remember was nearly 10/10ths. It was flying almost due south and was going to pass just west of the aerodrome. We turned towards it and set off in pursuit. As I was leading I got there first and after a short burst it dived into the ground about a mile or so south west of base. I am sure it must have been damaged further inland and was trying to limp home. With hindsight we could have forced it to land but the aerodrome had been badly bombed that morning and we all had a certain amount of desire for revenge and, anyhow, there was no way of telling before it was shot down that it was definitely in trouble. It might equally have been about to come below cloud to find the aerodrome before bombing it again.
>
> "An unusual feature of the event is that I had taken command of 601 Squadron on 16 August and I must be the only squadron commander to have shot down an enemy aircraft in full view of his squadron, both in the air and from the ground, and within an hour or so of being given command."

That "...certain amount of desire for revenge" is reflected, too, in the recollections of a 43 Squadron engine fitter, James Beedle, who later visited the crash site in the gardens of the house. When Beedle got there about a week later he found a flying boot with a leg still inside it and recalls it being consigned to the crater. "We didn't give a damn about them, actually," he later said "after all, the Germans had just bombed us to blazes!" It was a natural reaction, of course, and one that may well have resulted in deceased aircrew being given scant regard on frequent other occasions. However, no sign of the crew had been found when the crash site was excavated (at least twice) by the Wealden Aviation Archaeological Group, first in 1972 and again in 1978. (Shopwyke House was now a private school and had been renamed Westbourne House.)

On each occasion, attempts to salvage any of the buried wreckage were thwarted by a swimming-pool that had been constructed after the crash right across the crater. All that came to light, perhaps importantly, were portions of red and white paint that could be identified as remnants of the II./ZG 76 sharks-mouth emblem – paintwork traces that had also been significant in the Slackstead Farm Me 110 recovery. However, and whilst this had helped to tie the incident almost certainly to Lemmer and Lewandowski, it did not in any way help to explain what had happened to the two airmen. Ian Hutton, though, had a theory which he presented to the German War Graves Service in January 2001:

> "It is my belief that Lt Walter Lemmer was buried in Row U, Grave 1 at Portsdown Cemetery on 20 August 1940 as an 'Unknown Airman' killed on 16 August at South Mundham, West Sussex. I believe that the authorities made a mistake that day due to the large number of casualties. I believe that they mistakenly connected this unknown airman with a Ju 87 from 3./StG 2 which crash-landed at Bowley Farm, South Mundham, that day. The confusion arose, I suggest, because the bodies of the two deceased crew from that aeroplane became separated – Ofw Witt being dead at the scene and Fw Rocktaschel dying in hospital at Chichester the next day. Both of these men have known graves and are thus accounted for."

There is reason to suppose that the crew of the Shopwyke crash were Lt Walther Lemmer and Obgefr Josef Lewandowski although no obvious trace of burial for either man could be found in the immediate vicinity. Researcher Ian Hutton, however, theorised that an unknown Luftwaffe airman buried some miles away at Portsdown, Hampshire, must have been from the Shopwyke incident. Ian persuaded the German authorities that this man (now re-interred at Cannock Chase) must have been Walter Lemmer who is shown here. His grave, currently marked as an 'unknown', awaits its named headstone.

Certainly, it might be a credible explanation and when the German authorities checked their exhumation reports relating to the transfer of the body to Cannock Chase it was noted that the casualty at Portsdown in Row U, Grave 1, had been found to have "silver piping to his uniform". Given that the German authorities considered this piping could only have come from an officer's tunic*, and Walter Lemmer had indeed been an officer, the German War Graves Service wrote to Ian on 5 December 2001 confirming that they were satisfied this was indeed Walter Lemmer and would name his grave at Cannock Chase appropriately in due course. Whilst the link seemed somewhat tenuous, it was nonetheless accepted by the German authorities even though the death certificate for this casualty clearly records it as having occurred at Bowley Farm, South Mundham, some miles distant from Shopwyke. Even if one accepts that the casualty did *not* come from the crash of the Ju 87 at Bowley Farm then this would surely not automatically mean that the casualty *must* have come from Shopwyke or that it had been Lemmer.

What is certain is that there had been confusion in 1940, and making sense of the existing records more than sixty years later cannot be straightforward in this case. Yes, a strong possibility must exist that this casualty is Walter Lemmer. However, given that there were a number of other missing German casualties in the district at around this period there is nothing to say, surely, that it is merely the *place* of death that has been incorrectly logged? Some might reasonably argue that the stringent tests of reliability relating to the identification of this man might not have been met beyond reasonable doubt. Were this a commonwealth casualty then the evidence would certainly have been insufficient to identify him.

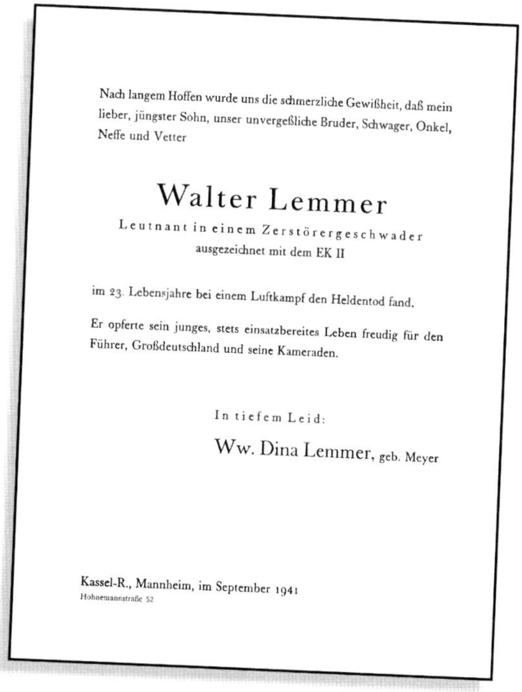

Nach langem Hoffen wurde uns die schmerzliche Gewißheit, daß mein lieber, jüngster Sohn, unser unvergeßliche Bruder, Schwager, Onkel, Neffe und Vetter

Walter Lemmer

Leutnant in einem Zerstörergeschwader

ausgezeichnet mit dem EK II

im 23. Lebensjahre bei einem Luftkampf den Heldentod fand.

Er opferte sein junges, stets einsatzbereites Leben freudig für den Führer, Großdeutschland und seine Kameraden.

In tiefem Leid:

Ww. Dina Lemmer, geb. Meyer

Kassel-R., Mannheim, im September 1941

Hohnemannstraße 52

Before Ian Hutton's intervention, Walter Lemmer's sole commemoration was probably this memorial card printed after his disappearance in 1940.

* In fact, and whilst silver piping as a braided cord was certainly applied to the collar edges of Luftwaffe officers it is also true that silver piping, in the form of an edging, was also applied to some Luftwaffe NCO uniform tunics. Those of Uffz rank and above being so marked. One must conclude that the German War Graves Service in this case were satisfied that the silver piping indeed denoted an officer's tunic and that they were not getting confused with what might have been an NCO's silver edging.

CHAPTER 10 The Lost Night Intruders

AS WE HAVE ALREADY seen, the families of many aircrews, formerly listed as missing, have been greatly comforted by the results of painstaking research which often leads to a former husband, son or brother being rescued from his undignified tomb to be accorded a decent burial. Such was the case with a Junkers 88 downed at Gedney Hill in Lincolnshire. The air intelligence report contained in The National Archives (file Air 22/267) records the loss of the Junkers 88 which crashed at Hurns Farm, just off French Drove at Gedney Hill near Peterborough and reads as follows:

> "Junkers 88. Crashed on 17 April 1941 at 21.23 hours at Hurns Farm, Thorney, near Ely. Map reference F.7828. No markings were visible and no plates were found, but one rubber cover of a petrol tank bore the date 1 November 1940. The cause of the crash is unknown; no fighter action appears to have taken place in the area and the aircraft is not claimed by AA. It appears to have been on fire in the air. The aircraft dived vertically into soft clay, is almost entirely buried and the crater is full of water. Pieces of an MG.15 were found and a few bits of armour, but no details possible. Crew; presumed 4, believed all killed in crash."

In fact, the statement by the RAF intelligence officer that all four crew members had been killed was incorrect. No doubt this presumption was based on the belief that the aircraft was the usual type of Junkers 88, a bomber carrying a crew of four men. However, in a 1977 letter to the Wealden Aviation Archaeological Group, which had become interested in the site, the Deutsche Dienstelle (WASt) the German records centre in Berlin, suggested that the aeroplane involved could well have been a Junkers Ju 88 C variant of the 4./NJG2, lost with its crew of three on 17 April 1941. Subsequent investigations indeed proved this to be the case, although the significance of its arrival on British soil had clearly been lost on RAF intelligence officers during 1941. It was, in fact, one of the very first Junkers 88 night fighters to fall on land over the United Kingdom, although the first intact example had come down near King's Lynn on 10 March 1941. The Gedney Hill Junkers would probably have revealed considerably less in the way of technical detail than its Norfolk counterpart, although the eventual excavation in 1978 did locate some items which would certainly have been of interest to RAF intelligence in 1941.

Following difficult negotiations for permission to excavate which involved the tenant farmer, Mr Ernest Hurn, the land agent and Trinity College, Cambridge, which owned the land, an investigation and metal detector survey was made of the field on Saturday 16 September 1978. At the end of an all-day search tiny fragments of the aircraft were found close to the road – a long way from the area of the crash which had been indicated by eyewitnesses. Despite the shortage of firm evidence, and only faint metal detector readings, an excavation was organised for the weekend of 7/8 October, employing the local plant hire firm of Messrs Thory's – the only operator in the area having a giant Hymac 580c with an extended 35-foot boom. From eyewitness and official reports, together with an assessment of the very soft soil type, it was felt that a mechanical excavator with a deep reach would be needed. The machine offered by Messrs Thory's was likely to be the only piece of equipment that might be capable of carrying out the potentially challenging recovery operation that had been planned.

The first few feet of excavation revealed absolutely nothing, and barely any sign of soil disturbance. Then, at about seven feet, a large timber railway sleeper was unearthed. Beneath it could be seen the glint of aluminium – which turned out to be a Luftwaffe NCO's belt buckle. At this depth there were clear signs of aircraft wreckage, and a pungent reek of fuel and oil. Following the trail downwards a mass of wreckage was unearthed throughout the day, including propellers, undercarriage assemblies, the tailwheel, oxygen cylinders and a crankshaft and pistons from one shattered engine. The quantity of wreckage recovered, it would be true to say, overwhelmed the recovery team. Clearly little had been salvaged in 1941 and almost the entire aeroplane, tailwheel forward, had gone into the ground.

Careful sorting revealed smaller and more interesting objects, including cockpit items, flares, a dinghy and also some firm evidence that the crew were still in the aeroplane. Remains of flying clothing indicated beyond doubt that three men had died, this proven by the remains of three pairs of flying boots. Further examination of the recovered wreckage and spoil heap revealed fragmentary human remains, and consequently the Peterborough City Police were notified at once, their coroner's officer attending to remove from the crash site the remains of the airmen and a quantity of ammunition which had been uncovered.

Obgefr Wilhelm Beetz, pilot of the 4./NJG 2 night-fighter Junkers 88 brought down at Gedney Hill in Cambridgeshire.

Found amongst the excavated wreckage of the Gedney Hill Junkers 88 was this Luftwaffe wireless operator's badge which must have belonged to Gefr Rudolf Kronika. Its distortion tells its own story.

Detailed examination of the items taken away by the Wealden group later revealed a quantity of interesting paperwork, including some documents which would have surely been welcomed by RAF Intelligence at the time. One listed RAF airfields in East Anglia, together with corresponding code letters. In addition, the strap from the first aid kit confirmed the Werke Nummer of the aircraft (0345) and a handkerchief bore the initials RK. Undoubtedly, then, this was the suspected aeroplane of 4/NJG2. Not only did the Werke Nummer correspond, but the initials RK would probably indicate its owner to have been Rudolf Kronika, the wireless operator. No identity discs or papers were found, and nothing firmly to establish the identities of the other two crewmen. By deduction, however, they were obviously the pilot, Obergefreiter Wilhelm Beetz, and the gunner, Johann Mittag. He, like Kronika, had held the rank of Gefreiter.

The information was communicated to the coroner's officer of Peterborough City Police and, simultaneously, to the German War Graves Service by the Wealden group. However, on 11 October 1978 Superintendent Les Braithwaite of the Peterborough Police announced that the coroner did not propose to hold an inquest and by 4 November the remains had been handed to the German authorities for burial at Cannock Chase. By this time the Germans had accepted the evidence presented to them and had also been sent the initialled handkerchief by the recovery team. Ultimately, the three airmen were named and buried in Block 8 of the German military cemetery in a single grave, beneath a headstone bearing the three names.

Official efforts in Germany to trace the relatives of the three men only succeeded in locating the family of Wilhelm Beetz, who still had a brother and sister living in Heide, West Germany. Attempts to trace the families of Kronika and Mittag having failed, it was concluded that they were deceased or else living in what was then communist East Germany. Even an article in the popular national German newspaper *Bild* raised no response from anyone who was related to or who even knew Mittag and Kronika. However, Gunter Meier writing from Celle revealed that he had learnt to fly before the war with 'Willi' Beetz, at Fliegerschule (Flying School) 52 in Halberstadt. Writing in December 1978 he recalled how he had shared a room with Willi and another trainee pilot, named Theo Gentsch, for two years before they finally completed their training and were posted to operational units. Gentsch and Meier were luckier than their colleague Beetz, both of them surviving the war, and with Meier becoming a post-war gliding champion in Lower Saxony.

In his letter he enquired if Beetz's gold signet ring had been found. This he described as being plain gold, with no initials engraved on it. It is believed that he wore this following his engagement on 1 April 1940 to a 'Fraulein Erika'. Little was known of Miss Erika by Willi's brother, Rudolf, or by his sister, Anni Bukowski, except that she had been the daughter of a police officer. Neither of them had met her, nor did the family have any contact with her after Willi's death. Unlike the case of Messerschmitt 109 pilot Werner Knittel, the gold ring was never found during the excavations although as we shall see later it seems very likely that this was picked up at the time of the crash.

However, a leather purse, believed to be Willi's, did come to light during the 1977 dig and contained a few coins, a locker key, and a train ticket to Breda (his unit was stationed at Gilze-Rijen in the Netherlands) along with an aircraft manufacturer's plate obviously taken from a Luftwaffe training aeroplane, a Klemm 35. Perhaps the value to him of this data plate was that he had taken it from an aeroplane on which he had flown his first solo. Or maybe it was from an aeroplane that he had crashed during his training? However, the significance of the mystery maker's label will probably remain unknown, as will the exact reason or cause for the loss of the Junkers 88 which could well have been through some failure or accident rather than by any hits from British defences.

Witnesses to the incident were few in this remote and sparsely populated area on the Lincolnshire/Cambridgeshire border, but all speak of the aircraft being on fire in the air. This was clearly recalled by the farmer, Ernest Hurn, and 75-year-old Horace Watson of Gedney Hill, who was interviewed at the time of the excavation. He still lived at his home in Chestnut Cottages from where he had seen the crash whilst about to leave for duty as air raid warden at nearby Thorney. Mr Watson recalled:

> "It was about 9.30 in the evening and I had just left the house on my bike when I heard a shrill whistling noise in the air. I saw some sparks, and then there was a great explosion across the fields, followed by a great blaze. I rushed over, but there was nothing anyone

could do. There was still a fire, with just a great hole in the earth and fragments scattered in all directions. I saw somebody in the road pick up what I thought was an incendiary bomb, so I grabbed it and threw it in the ditch. Nothing was ever got out. They just filled in the hole and left it – men and all. I think they tried to get something out, but abandoned it after very little effort."

With wartime censorship restrictions any reports about German aircraft crashes published in newspapers were necessarily guarded. However, the crash of this particular aircraft was covered in remarkable detail in one local newspaper, *The Advertiser*:

Nazi Plane Crashes Near Village
Wreckage and Remains of Crew Deeply Buried
Fierce Flames for Two Hours
Eyewitnesses' Story

'One of three enemy raiders which crashed during a night attack on this country on Thursday night, a German bomber with a crew of four (sic), came down in a field near a village.

'At one moment it was circling round the village, apparently flying normally at a great height. In the next moment it was diving headlong to earth. It narrowly missed the cross-country cables of the grid system and the engines buried themselves twenty-five feet in the ground. The port wing tip cut the telegraph wires and made a gap in the hedge adjoining the road. The petrol tanks burst and fires broke out over a radius of a quarter of a mile. There were few eye witnesses of the crash but they agree in describing it as "a tremendous thud".

'A lady told the authorities that she saw the door of the aircraft open and a great shower of sparks come out of the cabin.

'The aircraft was unapproachable until over two hours after it fell. The wreckage lay in a great hole about twenty feet across and was enveloped in fierce flames in which flares and tracer bullets and other ammunition were continually crackling. Village firemen played hoses on the fire, and when daylight broke all but the wings were below the surface of a deep pond.

'This made the work of salvage and identification more difficult and on Tuesday Police and RAF experts were still dragging the water in search of a clue to the identities of the crew. A small boy named Rogers found a gold ring which was identified as a wedding ring. All German husbands wear them, but to the disappointment of the officials this was the first they had ever seen without an inscription. Pieces of armour plating that protect the crew were hauled out after a struggle. They were as much as three men could carry. The compass was also found, battered and bent but still brilliantly luminous, by a cottager a quarter of a mile away.

'The rubber dinghy, so tough that it would require two horses pulling in opposite directions to pull it apart, was found in small pieces nearby. One of the Police drags was broken before part of the cockpit came up, the metal work painted with the bright yellow anti-corrosion substance used on aircraft that have to fly over the sea.

'Of course, there were human remains, pitiful relics whatever one thinks of our foe.

'First on the scene after the crash was Joe Tawn, an elderly cottager. "I heard a thundering great buzz through the house," he told an *Advertiser* reporter. "The furniture shook and the lamp shook, and I knew there was going to be a crash because I have heard one before. I heard a tremendous thud and ran out of doors. It was an amazing sight. In a field only a few hundred yards from my home was a great wall of flame. It stretched right across the road. My son Richard told me afterwards that he saw it from the town, nine miles away. Horace Watson the warden and Ted Sismey my next door neighbour followed me to the scene. Bullets were going off and every now and then there were bright lights from the flares which the aircraft carried. It was impossible that anyone could be alive in such a furnace. Frank Cooper was on the road near his bungalow, about the same distance as mine on the other side of the crash but I could not get to him past the wall of flame."

'Mr Cooper described how he was standing on the roadside outside his home and heard the aircraft flying at a great height. It seemed to be circling around normally.

"The bomber then suddenly began to fall at a terrific speed with a loud screeching noise. The impact when it hit the ground was terrific. Flames instantly leapt up from the wreckage which was

A few pathetic effects were in Willi Beetz's wallet, although the most unusual was surely a data plate from a Klemm 35 trainer. Most likely it was a trophy he had retained from his days as a trainee pilot.

This photograph depicting a belly-landed Klemm 35 trainer was found on a Luftwaffe prisoner of war captured in Britain. It is tempting to speculate whether or not this is the very same Klemm from which Beetz collected his personal souvenir!

> unapproachable. A local policeman was here in ten minutes and the Home Guard and Special Constables and Wardens made a thorough search for any parachutists but it was impossible for anyone to have left the aircraft as it all happened so suddenly.'

The report gives us a vivid impression of the event and its aftermath, and is also interesting in that it would seem very likely that the young lad Rogers had discovered the ring belonging to Wilhelm Beetz, and about which Willi Meir had enquired many years later. Its description would certainly fit that given by Meir, and its lack of any inscription is certainly noteworthy. What might have happened to that ring, possibly the one given to Willi by Fraulein Erica, can now only remain speculation.

Last word must go to the family in Germany who were pleased and touched that, at long last, their brother Willi had been found and buried. Writing in January 1979, his brother Rudolf noted that 'the news of the discovery has touched me deeply and occupied me a lot. I have thought long and hard with melancholy and sadness about the best sons of our land who sacrificed themselves in good faith. Those terrible years took away so many young men, amongst them our Willi. Both my sister and I have been pleased to know, after so long, what happened to our dear brother. Now we are happy that before we die we may go to see his last resting place and we thank you for all your efforts. I am sure that this is what Willi and his comrades would have wanted.'

It is a commonly expressed sentiment, and one that time and again has been made by the relatives of previously missing aircrew. It is also a sentiment that consistently underlines that the proper and reverent removal, identification and burial of the wartime missing is almost always the appropriate course of action. As this book goes to print, scores of British and Commonwealth dead, missing since the First World War, are being identified and buried in a newly constructed cemetery at Fromelles, France. Nobody would surely deny that this is right and proper, even after such a long period of time.

CHAPTER 11 The Mystery of Reekes Wood

THE MYSTERY SURROUNDING THE loss of a Dornier 217 during the early hours of the night of 8 March 1943 could and should have been resolved during August 1989. Instead, it took another sixteen years before the puzzle was finally unravelled during the summer of 2005. That mystery surrounded the disappearance of twenty-one-year-old crew member, Obgefr Franz Huske. As with many accounts relating to the discovery of missing wartime aircrew in Britain during post-war years, it is yet another tale that has more than its fair share of controversy and intrigue.

It was during the late hours of 7 March 1943 that five heavily laden Dornier 217s from the 1st Staffel of Kampfgeschwader 2 took off from their Dutch base at Gilze-Rijen airfield and headed for Southampton docks. The gaggle of bombers droned out of their base into the darkness at two-minute intervals, although the aeroplane of specific interest in this account was U5 + EH, Werke Nummer 5526, flown by Fw Günter Vestewig. Writing during the late 1970s to researcher Chris Goss, Vestewig takes up the story:

Obgefr Franz Huske, the air gunner on board the I/KG 2 Dornier 217 shot down at Fernhurst, West Sussex, on the night of 7/8 March 1943. Huske remained missing until June 2005.

"The attack height was to be 4,000 metres (approx 12,000ft) against what were assumed to be large ships of the English fleet, and against which a steep gliding attack was to be carried out. We reached our start position on the French coast a little early and at an altitude of 1,500 metres and to take up the time I went on a westerly course and then an easterly course back to the start position from the French coast. From here, I rose up to 4,000 metres flying on a northerly course. We flew over the English coast, and then further inland with the intention of reaching Southampton on a southerly course. Suddenly, there were sparks and flashes in the cockpit and the sounds of glass breaking. The radio stopped working and between the starboard engine and the fuselage we could see flames. Then we could see flames coming from the starboard engine. I turned the plane on its back and nose-dived to extinguish the flames and the fire got smaller. When I pulled the plane out of the dive the flames were bigger than ever. Now, I couldn't keep the Dornier level and we flew in a downward curve to the left. The possibility of reaching the French coast was nil, and the danger of explosion was too great. I gave the order 'Bale out!' and my navigator disconnected the radio cable on my flying helmet to save me from strangling myself.

"I assume that we were hit by two bursts from a night fighter, and that explains the loss of life (two of the crew were killed in the night-fighter attack) and the sparks and shattered glass and Perspex in the cockpit and the burning wing. What happened afterwards cannot be reported objectively but the fact is that my radio operator is buried at Chichester and my flight engineer has never been found (sic). My navigator was wounded in the nose and chin by shrapnel and in his left hand and knee. I was seriously wounded with a fractured skull, broken ribs and a shot through my shin bone. When I was hanging on my parachute – I have no recall of it opening – I had a curious and strange sensation that I was somehow gliding above the well-lit Olympic stadium of Berlin in 1936. Surely that could not be possible? Then I noticed the swinging of the parachute before it touched the ground. I landed in a clearing in the woods. Every time I regained consciousness I shouted for help. How long it lasted I just don't know.

"Suddenly, there were soldiers. One of them took off his jacket and vest. They poured tea from a flask onto the clothing and used it to clean my bloodstained face. When I became conscious again I was at a farm. There I was lying on a stretcher and an old man with a lamp was standing over me. He had very long hair, which was unusual in those days, and he stroked me gently saying 'My dear son, my dear son'. I eventually regained consciousness on a hospital operating table. I remember saying 'Does the leg stay on?' Well, the leg stayed on but I got a replacement silver shin."

Günter Vestewig was correct in his assumption that the attack had come from a night fighter, and this in fact was a West Malling-based Beaufighter of 29 Squadron, flown by Sqn Ldr G H Goodman with his radar operator, Fg Off W F E Thomas. The combat report from the crew provides a brutal contemporary account of the engagement which triggered the events covered in this chapter:

"Took off from West Malling at 00.30 hours and landed at 01.50 hours on 8 March 1943. The Beaufighter was controlled by Sector (Controller: Flt Lt Webber) and told to orbit

> Beacon 'L' at 12,000 ft. Were given 'Smack' almost immediately south and a contact obtained at maximum range at 12,000ft altitude on an aircraft slightly below and to port. The target was jinking violently and was chased for about five minutes south west. A visual was then obtained at 350 yards range and was identified at 200 yards as a Dornier 217. The Beaufighter opened fire at 150 yards range on the target, which was still jinking, giving a three second burst with cannon and machine gun. A large explosion was seen on the inboard of the port engine. The Beaufighter drew away slightly to port and then closed in again at 140 mph as the aircraft lost speed and giving a further three to four second burst when another violent explosion was seen. The aircraft practically stalled and the Beaufighter had to climb steeply to avoid a collision. The pilot then saw a large fire and explosions on the ground approximately to the south west of the Horsham area at about 00.48 hours. One Do 217 claimed as destroyed."

As Günter Vestewig drifted down on his parachute, hallucinating that he was over the Berlin olympic stadium, his Dornier slammed vertically into the ground below him at Reekes Wood on Vann Common, Fernhurst, in West Sussex. With him, Obegefr Gerhard Polzin had parachuted into captivity but the radio operator, Obegefr Hans Witkopp fell with an unopened parachute. Of the fourth crew member, Obegefr Franz Huske, there was no trace – leading the RAF air intelligence officers to conclude "....it seems probable that his body is in the wreckage". As we shall see, it was an accurate assumption.

From the buried and scattered wreckage, little of any value or interest could be gleaned by the RAF investigators, and whilst unexploded bombs were found shortly after the crash at nearby Cartref Farm and Amos Copse it was clear from these finds that they did not represent the normal full complement of bombs one might expect to find on board an aircraft of this type. All the same, if any other bombs were still on board then they were assessed to be deeply buried along with the wreckage. Certainly, there had on impact been an explosion in the wreckage but this was most certainly fuel rather than ordnance. In any event, it was relatively uncommon for Luftwaffe bomb loads to detonate on impact during a crash. This was due to the fact that the electrical arming of the bombs meant the bomb fuses had to be 'charged' electrically before release. Since this had not happened in the Fernhurst incident, any bombs in the aircraft would have effectively been unable to detonate with the crash. However, it was not long before the buried wreckage, any bomb load contained within it and the fate of the unfortunate Franz Huske were all forgotten. Forgotten, that is, until the upsurge in the activity of amateur investigations of wartime aircraft wrecks that began to flourish in the 1970s.

During that period the Fernhurst crash was investigated and part-excavated by a team including Peter Dimond and teenager Chris Goss (now Wing Commander Goss) who located the shallow depression and scattered alloy debris which marked the exact point of impact in the wood. At this particular time there existed no requirement to seek Ministry of Defence authority for excavations of this nature, and the team of enthusiasts dug at the site over a period of weekends. Ultimately, the heavy clay and a serious ingress of water defeated them. It was clear that the bulk of the wreckage lay buried much deeper and way

The crater caused by the crashing Dornier in Reekes Wood, photographed during 1989.

out of reach. Access to the site by mechanical excavator was, then, pretty much impossible and therefore this was not an option. However, amongst items recovered were bits of a Luftwaffe NCO's uniform belt and a holstered Belgian-manufactured Browning FN 9mm pistol. Finds of this nature pointed strongly to the likelihood that its original owner was probably not far away. In this case it would have been Franz Huske.

With the impossibility of continuing any further effective excavations at the site, the tentative investigations commenced by Peter Dimond and Chris Goss were abandoned and nature was left to take over once again. It wasn't long before the crater became filled with stagnant water and after the big storm of October 1987 that struck south-east England, fallen trees had added to nature's camouflage. In any event, others who had subsequently gone calling on the landowner for permission to investigate the site were told in no uncertain terms that she wished it to remain undisturbed. The stance of the landowner and the implementation in 1986 of the Protection of Military Remains Act surely meant that the Dornier, and Franz Huske, would remain lost forever, deep in the claggy clay soil beneath a thick blanket of vegetation. As far as the MOD were concerned, no licence would ever be granted for work on a site where it was expected that missing aircrew might be present. Events, however, then took a quite surprising turn.

During 1988, and in the course of detailed research into wartime air losses over the county of Sussex, the author established contact with the sister of Franz Huske in what was then communist East Germany. Charlotte Schilde was both astonished and relieved to get news from England as to the fate of her brother and wrote as follows to the author:

The crash site is surveyed by a team including Peter Dimond and (crouching) the author in 1989. On this visit a 50kg bomb fin was found and is being held by the author (right).

> "I still cannot really grasp that the wreck of the aircraft containing the remains of my brother has been found after forty-five years. How much we had always hoped that sometime we should hear something because he had not been found. Also, the Red Cross was unable to tell us anything of the whereabouts of my brother. It is such a pity that my parents are not still living. He was their only son and, above all, to my mother he was especially dear. She died five years ago.
>
> "I too loved my brother dearly, and the news after forty-five years that you know where he lies is just as painful as when we received the news that he had not returned from an attack. On 14 December 1943 he was finally declared dead by the Luftwaffe. Now, I am most grateful that you have given me this news of my brother. I hope it will be possible that his remains should eventually be buried where his friend Hans Witkopp lies."

It was an all-too-familiar story; the family knowing nothing, a long desire for news....and when it finally came that news being too late to be of any comfort to an adoring mother. However, the fact that Charlotte Schilde had now received confirmation concerning the *whereabouts* of her brother was a very long way removed from her hoped-for reality of seeing him buried with his comrade, Hans Witkopp. Notwithstanding the desire of the family to have Franz found, identified and decently buried it was unfortunately the case that things were not quite that simple. As we have already seen, the stance of the landowner and the likely refusal of any request for a recovery licence from the MOD might yet conspire against the wishes of Frau Schilde for her brother to be laid to rest.

Following up Charlotte Schilde's request for further information, the author visited the crash site during the spring of 1989 in company with Peter Dimond who had excavated there fifteen years or more previously. Guided to the site by Peter, the author found still scattered around the impact crater signs that an aircraft had crashed here; fragments of airframe structure, Perspex, engine components and exploded rounds of ammunition. There was, however, one other discovery during that particular site visit that might yet be the key to finding Franz Huske – albeit in a rather roundabout way. Lying on the edge of the crater, now full of stinking green stagnant water, was an apparently insignificant triangular sheet of rusty steel. In fact, it was a sheared fin from a German 50kg bomb.

Given that the bombs that had fallen at the time of the crash in nearby Amos Copse, and at Cartref Farm, could not have comprised the entire complement of bombs on board, and that we know Günter Vestewig had not dropped any of his bombs before baling out, it was not unreasonable to conclude that the biggest part of the Dornier bomb load must surely remain buried on site, intermingled with the wreckage and any bodily remains of the unfortunate Franz Huske. Whilst it was an interesting discovery, the find of the bomb fin did not initially help to take forward any possible recovery of Franz Huske. If anything it hindered any such plans. Hindered, that is, unless the problem of making any progress was given a little more applied thought and lateral thinking.

Surely, the author concluded, the bomb fin was a pretty good indicator that one and possibly more of the bombs on board the Dornier 217 were still buried at the site? This being the case then maybe the authorities could now be persuaded to act. After all, the bombs (if they were there) were in reasonable proximity to nearby habitation. In fact, the wood in which they were possibly buried was now part of the extended garden of a large detached private house; Hambledon. In all probability the best part of a 4,000kg bomb load lay buried just yards away from the unsuspecting occupants. Given that this might not be a very satisfactory state of affairs for the future, the author alerted the RAF bomb disposal unit (explosive ordnance disposal or EOD) to the discovery of the fin. Maybe, after all, if an official attempt was made to recover the bombs then, as a by-product almost, the remains of Franz Huske might also be recovered.

Certainly, any buried bomb load might be expected to be deeper than the wreck of the Dornier with its unfortunate occupant. The momentum of impact would have driven the stowed missiles onwards and deeper. Thus, recovering the bombs would definitely mean first of all removing the wreckage above them, along with its still-missing crew member.

By the spring of 1989 the RAF's EOD team, under the supervision of Wing Commander Keith Hopkins, had negotiated with the landowner to investigate the crash site with a view to recovering and making safe the bomb load that was now suspected to be present. Under the circumstances, the landowner needed precious little persuasion to be convinced that an excavation there by the RAF bomb disposal experts might be a sensible course of action. However, and whilst the discovery of Franz Huske's remains seemed highly likely it was disappointing that on 3 May 1989 Wing Commander Hopkins wrote, stating: "Our responsibility is limited to explosive ordnance recovery. We would not wish to disturb human remains unless they were in the way of such recovery." Nevertheless, and as set out above,

During the RAF's excavation of the site in 1989 the remaining bomb load of the Dornier 217 was retrieved. Here, an unexploded 500kg weapon is hauled out on the digger bucket under RAF supervision.

it was unlikely that any bombs could be reached without first finding the missing man. They would therefore, surely, be "...in the way of such recovery". That, at least, was not an unreasonable conclusion and there therefore seemed to be a very reasonable chance indeed that quite possibly Charlotte Schilde's wishes could at last be met as the result of official action. Unfortunately, when that action finally came during August 1989 it did not have the hoped-for results – at least insofar as Franz Huske was concerned.

Between 14 and 26 August of that year the RAF Wittering-based EOD team worked at the crash site in Fernhurst, although the excavations had to be undertaken by a locally-hired private mechanical excavator and driver – the RAF's own JCB having been declared unsafe through corrosion just prior to the operation. Already, magnetometer surveys had indicated the presence of buried 'targets' that were most likely bombs and those findings were vindicated when, at fifteen feet, the first unexploded bomb (a 50kg weapon) was unearthed. Associated with this bomb were the long bomb-bay support girders and most of the bomb-bay floor. In order to facilitate the recovery of the bombs all of the buried wreckage, including an engine and propeller blade, was hauled out by the JCB as excavations then continued down to a depth of twenty-five feet. At this depth the final bombs were found – in total, five 50kg weapons and two 500kg bombs had been recovered, thus making this the largest single post-war haul of unexploded bombs ever dealt with by RAF EOD teams. At least one of the bombs was found to have an anti-removal

device although ultimately all of the bombs were rendered safe. As we shall see, the discovery of the bomb-bay flooring would, much later, take on a very special significance.

What we know from the EOD internal report of 31 August 1989 is that the wreckage was all re-buried on site on conclusion of the extraction of the bombs. This was carried out once the excavation had been declared cleared of all metallic readings that might indicate the presence of further weapons. Consequently, it was first necessary to ensure that the excavation was 'clean' before the final checks and survey were carried out. Once satisfied that nothing further remained, the several tons of wreckage that had been brought to the surface were then consigned back into the pit before it was back-filled and

The bomb load was neutralised and steamed-out on site. First, each weapon had to be carefully checked by stethoscope for anti-handling devices or ticking fuses.

After the RAF explosive ordnance team had completed work on the site they placed this memorial plaque to Franz Huske on an adjacent tree. The plaque is no longer there, and had vanished not long after it had been erected.

made good. This included the bomb-bay girders and flooring. Officially, no trace of Franz Huske had been found.

By October of that year the author was pressing Wing Commander Hopkins about the disappearance of Obegefr Huske, although the response reiterated that the EOD brief was simply to recover the unexploded ordnance and not to concern or involve themselves with human remains unless they hampered or impeded the EOD operation. In writing, he later stated officially that: "Our task was to deal with unexploded ordnance and only to become involved with human remains if they impeded our operation. Consequently, I ensured that the status quo was maintained at the end of our operation." Unofficially, and in a subsequent handwritten note, he added: "As you may know, my 'official' view cannot always be the same as my private one. I am sure you understand!"

Quite what happened in the case of Franz Huske remained, at that time, a complete mystery and to the author it seemed inconceivable that he had not been found. However, there was another twist in the saga when on 1 November 1989 the RAF Wittering EOD returned to the site and placed a small memorial plaque to the memory of Frank Huske over the original crater. For Charlotte Schilde the outcome was not as she had hoped, but as far as the author was aware she was never contacted by the authorities to tell her of the excavation or its outcome and neither was she informed about the RAF's memorial plaque. After all, nothing had changed. Franz Huske was still missing. The "status quo" to which Wing Commander Keith Hopkins had more than once referred had most certainly been maintained.

To all intents and purposes the case of Franz Huske ended when the RAF EOD team left the site on 26 August 1989 and a line had certainly been drawn under the matter with the low-key delivery to the site of the memorial plaque on 1 November 1989. There seemed little chance, now, that Franz Huske would ever be found although those involved in the UK aviation archaeology movement were deeply suspicious of what had transpired here. It simply beggared belief that absolutely *no* trace of Huske had been discovered during the recovery of the bombs. And yet that was the official line.

Curiosity, though, soon got the better of various individuals and it was not long before the plant hire operator used by the RAF had surreptitiously returned to the site with his JCB to brazenly (and unofficially!) dig out one of the BMW 801 engines that he knew had been left there because he had been instructed to re-bury it. He evidently did so under the pretence of completing the site reinstatement but making off with his prize he left the site with bits of debris and wreckage now obviously at or near the surface. Again, it wasn't long before other interested individuals went back to the site to have yet another look. After all, the attendant publicity surrounding the discovery of the bombs had been significant. It was hardly a secret. What these other unauthorised visitors found at the site where the plant operator had again churned things over was both astonishing and surprising. Large portions of uniform tunic, a watch, lucky charm, belt, bracelet or necklace, parts of a Mae West and a Luftwaffe side-cap eagle were all found with some of the wreckage previously buried after the EOD operation. Doing anything about it would be difficult if not impossible, especially given the landowner's original position and the memorial plaque now over the site. The RAF operation had effectively closed off all future options. Once more, though, there would be another twist.

By 2005 the previous landowner had gone, and Hambledon and its rambling garden and wood now came into the hands of a new owner who was concerned that wreckage and possibly human remains had been left on his property – although by this time there was no longer any trace of the memorial plaque left by the RAF in 1989. Consequently, a team from Tangmere Military Aviation Museum applied for and were granted a licence to re-excavate the site in the summer of 2005.That a licence was granted at all can only be regarded as surprising since the MOD will not ordinarily grant one for a recovery operation where any member of the crew is still unaccounted for. Later, the MOD would tell the press that they had no idea there were any remains on site, but then rather contradictorily went on to state: "It is MOD policy not to grant a licence for a dig where it is believed there is a body buried. In this case there were special circumstances because of the landowner's request." It was a statement that rather flew in the face of the MOD's assertion that they had no idea Huske's remains were present on site; in the same breath they had also stated that this was the very reason for the granting of an excavation licence. Quite possibly, however, it was the RAF's excavations at the site in 1989 that had now given the MOD confident although misplaced reassurance to grant a recovery licence to the Tangmere team in 2005.

Whilst the MOD perhaps did not know Huske's remains were still at the site, the team from Tangmere certainly had good reason to believe that they were. So too did the new landowner. Indeed, the over-riding purpose of this fresh recovery was to find and recover Franz Huske. Consequently, it was hardly a surprise when his remains were found in the wreckage of the bomb bay at a depth of twenty-two feet by the Tangmere Museum team over the weekend of 11/12 June 2005. It was the same bomb bay that had been re-buried there by the RAF EOD team.

Quite what had happened during the 1989 operation it is difficult to establish. Wing Commander Keith Hopkins has since died, and it has been impossible to find any of the original RAF team from that operation twenty-one years ago. There are, though, only two possibilities. The first is that the EOD team simply didn't see or notice the remains during their dig at the site and then unknowingly re-buried them with the wreckage. The second and rather controversial scenario is that the remains were *deliberately* re-buried to maintain

Visits to the site by unauthorised persons after the RAF had completed their operations in 1989 resulted in the discovery of large portions of uniform, flying clothing and personal effects that could only have belonged to Franz Huske.

The headstone to Obgefr Hans Witkopp in Chichester Cemetery. He was the radio operator on board the Fernhurst Dornier and his comrade Franz Huske now lies buried alongside him.

what Keith Hopkins had so pointedly called the status-quo. Whichever it was there can be absolutely no doubt at all that the RAF team *had* re-buried the remains, whether by accident or design. However, it almost beggars belief that those remains were not noticed during the course of that excavation. Either way, it all came too late for Charlotte Schilde who had passed away in the intervening years. After an inquest by West Sussex Coroner Roger Stone during November 2005, and when Huske was formally identified and named, the young Luftwaffe flier was laid to rest at Portfield Cemetery, Chichester, during October 2006 close to his friend Hans Witkopp exactly as his sister had wished.

When the Tangmere recovery team sifted and cleaned the staggering two tons of wreckage retrieved during the 2005 operation they discovered a torch, a Schnapps bottle and an unbroken bottle of perfume from Marseille. Perhaps the latter was intended as a gift for Franz's girlfriend, or maybe for his adoring mother or much-loved sister, Charlotte? Either way, its intended recipient never received it and both the mother and sister of Franz Huske passed away without ever knowing that finally their beloved Franz was at rest.

CHAPTER 12

The Middlesbrough Dornier

WITHOUT EXCEPTION ALL OF the other losses covered in this book are those where the recoveries were planned and intentional, but the case of a Dornier 217 brought down at South Bank, Cleveland, on 15 January 1942 is both different and unusual. Its discovery, and that of one of its crew members, was entirely unplanned and accidental and arose out of work being carried out by the Northumbrian Water Board to lay sewers for a new business park development. It was on 26 November 1997 that the contractor's machinery crunched into buried wreckage and a fascinating tale began to unfold.

Ofw Heinrich Richter, the air gunner on board the Dornier 217 brought down at Middlesbrough on 15 January 1942.

During the late afternoon of 15 January 1942, Dornier 217 aircraft of KG 2 were tasked with attacking British shipping and harbour installations along the east coast, and in an operation flown from Schipol in the Netherlands around twelve Dornier 217s set out for Britain's north-east coastline. One of the aircraft was U5 + HS, Werke Nummer 5314, of 8./KG 2 flown by Fw Joachim Lehnis with his crew of Lt Rudolf Matern (observer/bomb aimer), Uffz Hans Maneke (radio operator) and Ofw Heinrich Richter (air gunner). As they flew towards Tees Bay off Middlesbrough the crew spotted a single coaster riding at anchor directly ahead of them. Almost without looking they had immediately stumbled across a target of opportunity that fell within their mission brief and the crew readied themselves at once for the run-in to attack the coaster.

The vessel was in fact the SS *Empire Bay* on a voyage from Hartlepool to London with its cargo of coal. At around 18.15 hours her crew had been alerted to a likely impending raid by the sound of air raid sirens wailing on shore and eventually spotted the single Dornier heading straight for them and at not more than two hundred feet. On board the Dornier, Lt Matern peered through his bombsight before releasing a stick of bombs which straddled the *Empire Bay*. Although she was only a coaster,

This was the scene at South Bank station, Middlesbrough, after the impact of the Dornier 217 onto the railway lines on 15 January 1942.

the *Empire Bay* was far from defenceless and had on board Royal Navy DEMS gunners who gave retaliatory fire from their Lewis guns. Whilst the target was fast it was also low and close and the gunners claimed to have registered some hits on their attacker as it flew over them and towards the land. As it headed away from the *Empire Bay* the Dornier 217 was seen to be losing height and trailing a plume of black smoke. Perhaps at this point the Dornier was not yet fatally crippled, although as it crossed the coastline it flew directly towards 938 Barrage Balloon Squadron's Tees protective cordon.

Moments later it had impacted with the taut steel cable of one of the balloons and instantly plunged earthwards. At such a low altitude there could be no hope of escape for the four men on board before it eventually smashed into a double-track railway siding by South Bank railway station. The force of the impact threw wreckage far and wide, tore up the railway lines, scattered the track ballast and blasted a deep crater beneath which the bulk of the wreckage was deeply buried. Investigators picking over the pitiful remains found little of any significant intelligence to report upon but discovered the mutilated bodies of three German airmen who were duly removed for burial.

Meanwhile, and since this was an important industrial railway siding, the priority was to repair the track and get the lines working again. Consequently, engineers rapidly in-filled the crater and re-laid the ballast and track, having the permanent way open again in a matter of days. It wasn't long before the locomotives and wagons were rumbling over the site again, although with one crew man unaccounted for it seemed highly likely that he must still be beneath the tracks. Given the location it also seemed likely that this would be his permanent resting place.

In 1942, however, little thought was probably given to the unfortunate soul who had been lost and forgotten in this the most ignominious of places. Meanwhile, the SS *Empire Bay* had also been fatally wounded with her plates blasted and buckled below the water line. Although she had taken no direct hits, the blast and the pressure waves of bombs bursting just beneath the water alongside her had done their work and she settled stern-first onto the seabed with her anchor chains straining taut from the bow. Eventually, she slipped under the waves and became a total wreck although thankfully without any loss of life. With the *Empire Bay* gone and the railway tracks repaired it was inevitable that life, and the war, would move on. Both were soon forgotten. However, it would be true to say that the crash site of the Dornier 217 did attract curiosity in later years of hopeful aviation archaeologists, although any chances of digging there were clearly thwarted in view of its location. Thwarted, that is, until events during the autumn of 1997.

When the accidental discovery of the wreckage was made it was clear that a considerable quantity of metal lay buried there and the contractors were clearly perplexed, if not a little worried, by what it was they had stumbled upon. Of course, it quickly became apparent that this was the wreckage of a German bomber and very soon local residents were doubtless able to confirm that this was indeed where a Dornier 217 had plunged to its destruction in 1942. All but forgotten in the intervening years, the crash had left no physical scars to show the point of impact. Nonetheless, this was a bomber aircraft and that meant one thing; there could still be unexploded bombs there.

During excavations at the crash site in 1997 this Oberfeldwebel's rank collar patch was discovered.

Consequently, and following the involvement of the local police, the RAF's 5131 Explosive Ordnance Disposal Unit from RAF Wittering were tasked to attend and deal with the buried wreckage. This was in line with service protocols which require that RAF units are required to deal with unexploded ordnance associated with aircraft wrecks on land. However, there was no way of knowing at this stage whether any bombs *were* present and the RAF EOD team's role was precautionary and not based upon any knowledge that bombs were indeed on site. However, there were other issues too that needed to be considered. First, there was the question of removing several tons of wrecked aircraft out of the developer's way and, of course, this might well contain cannon or other small calibre ammunition in any case. Second, there was the issue of the crew. Certainly there were four men on board the aircraft when it had crashed, although only three of them had been found and buried in named graves at Thornaby. This begged the question; was there still a missing airman trapped in the wreckage?

Also discovered was this Unteroffizier's rank patch. These two discoveries enabled the missing crew man to be identified and buried and for a discrepancy in the naming of a previously buried casualty from this incident to be rectified.

When 5131 EOD Unit took over the digging from the contractors an overwhelming quantity of material emerged from the soil. In total, there was more than five tons of it. The haul included propeller blades, oleo legs and a landing wheel, machine guns, ammunition, two parachutes, a Revi gunsight, dinghy and a bomb rack……but no bombs. However, when shreds of Luftwaffe uniform material and a small number of human bones were discovered this gave added credence to the belief that the fourth and missing crew member might be in the wreckage. They dug deeper and more significant evidence of human remains was found. At once, a conclusion was reached; these must belong to the pilot, Fw Joachim Lehnis, since he was the only crew member not yet accounted for. Apparently confirming this supposition was the discovery of a collar rank tab of a yellow patch with three eagles and a silver border. In other words, the rank markings for a Feldwebel and there was only one man of this rank on board; the pilot. However, any certainty as to the identification of the remains being those of Lehnis were short lived when, on forensic examination, the collar rank tabs turned out to be those of an Oberfeldwebel. The fourth eagle presented a problem, since this would indicate the wearer had been Ofw Heinrich Richter. However, Richter was one of the crew members who had already been buried – as indeed had Lehnis. The only missing man was Uffz Maneke and indeed another discovery on the excavation had been yet another rank tab, this time for an Unteroffizier. Again, there was only man of this rank on board.

Faced with this conundrum, and unhelpfully with an identity disc that had been found but was too corroded to make any sense, a coroner's inquest held at Tesside during June 1998 concluded that the remains were, in fact, those of Ofw Heinrich Richter with the coroner further ruling that Maneke had originally been buried under Richter's name. The truth of the matter, of course, was that the nature of the crash and the unfortunately jumbled remains of both aeroplane and its crew had led to confusion in 1942 just as it had in 1997. What mattered, however, was that the entire crew of four had clearly been accounted for and certainly the discovery of the Unteroffizier's rank tab during the 1997 recovery drew a line under that. However, and following the coroner's ruling, the headstone to Richter was removed on 13 October 1998 and marked with a new headstone to Maneke. On the following day Richter was buried alongside his comrades and his headstone re-located over his grave. It had been a confused and convoluted chain of events, but one that eventually saw the entire crew reunited and appropriately named.

Attending the funeral service had been Heinz-Georg Möllenbrok who maintained during his lifetime a keen interest in matters appertaining to missing Luftwaffe aircrew, most especially from his old unit KG 2. Indeed, it will be seen as a common thread running throughout this book that there were a high percentage of cases involving missing airmen from that unit. Given that this Luftwaffe bomber unit was consistently involved in air operations against the British Isles from 1940 through to 1944 that is perhaps hardly surprising, particularly in view of the high number of losses sustained by them. As Herr Möllenbrok pointed out to the assembled news media: "Our Gruppe lost over two hundred and fifty aircraft and over three hundred and fifty aircrew were killed or posted missing in operations over England. It was a heavy price to pay."

After laying a wreath at the grave of Richter and his crew, Möllenbrok spoke warmly of his impressions gained at the burial service and of his surprise that so many local people had turned out to pay their respects to a former enemy. "I attribute this attitude to the sense of fair play which the British soul enshrines," he said. Certainly, a great deal of official effort had been expended in this case to see that the right thing was done and that the men were correctly identified and named. Sadly, no living relatives of these crew members could be found. Unfortunately, it is difficult not to contrast this case with that of the crash site at Fernhurst which is covered in the previous chapter. That instance also involved a Dornier 217, coincidentally it was also from KG 2, and it had a missing crew member on board. It also involved the official input of an RAF bomb disposal unit. Had things turned out differently as the result of that operation then the case of that missing man, Franz Huske, might well have been resolved many years before the site was re-excavated by the Tangmere Military Aviation Museum.

The case of the South Bank Dornier 217 crew was one of the last occasions when missing Luftwaffe personnel have been recovered within the United Kingdom prior to the publication of this book. There are, however, many wartime German aircraft crash sites where potential exists for such discoveries yet to be made.

CHAPTER 13 A Far from Ordinary Pond

THE AVERAGE VISITOR TO Eastbourne's Shinewater Park situated in the Langney district on the outskirts of the Sussex coastal town would hardly give a second glance at one of the many water features within the confines of the park. A roughly circular pond encompassed by a paling fence and supporting the usual flora and fauna of the wetland terrain hardly stands out as in any way unusual. Nothing suggests it to be anything other than just a natural feature. On a daily basis dozens of hikers, children going to school or to the nearby swings, ambling dog-walkers and energetic joggers all pass by – most of them certainly unaware of the violent and tragic circumstances that gave rise to this particular pond's existence. Its tranquillity belies the wartime violence that had created it.

To the residents of Eastbourne, by no means unused to aerial attack, the sound at about quarter to eleven on the night of 8 November 1943 was terrifyingly close. First, above the high altitude drone of aero engines, there was a short thump-thump-thump of cannon fire that reverberated through the miserably dark and rainy night. It was followed almost immediately by the increasing crescendo roar of a diving aeroplane, with engines at full throttle, and a cacophony of noise that seemed to go on for minutes. To many on the ground it seemed likely that they were about to be subjected to some kind of nocturnal dive-bombing attack. The climax, when it came, was a sudden and earth shaking thud...followed momentarily by near silence. The screaming engines had been stopped dead in an instant. Then, seconds later and away out to the north of the town near the Hampden Park district, a brilliant flash was followed by a thunderclap explosion that echoed off the South Downs and rolled back across the town, rattling roofs and windows in its wake. Whatever it was had impacted with an awful finality into the marshland sitting just to the west of Friday Street. However, the winter darkness and waterlogged nature of the land, criss-crossed with its numerous drainage dykes, made any investigation impossible until first light.

By dawn it was apparent that something fairly cataclysmic had occurred in the middle of Shinewater Marsh, on cattle grazing land then belonging to David Vine of Morning's Mill Farm at Willingdon. The scene that met the gaze of the first investigators arriving when daylight finally broke was one of unbelievable destruction and carnage. There, in the corner of a field, a vast crater had been blown out – approximately one hundred feet across and estimated at about forty feet deep at its centre. Thrown up all around were huge clods of

This was the scene of devastation after the impact and explosion of the Messerschmitt 410 that had been shot down onto Shinewater Marsh near Eastbourne on the night of 8/9 November 1943. It is easy to understand from this photograph how aircrew involved in such incidents simply disappeared.

blue clay and with the bottom of the huge crater now quite rapidly filling up with oil-flecked water. Strewn about the whole of the marsh were tiny fragments of aluminium alloy and items clearly recognisable as mangled aircraft parts. Intermingled with the scattered mud and wreckage were rather ghastly and grisly finds as more and more mutilated portions of body came to light across adjacent farmland.

Like many young schoolboys, eleven-year-old Richard Hassell was drawn to the crash scene as if it were some kind of magnet. When he arrived on his quest for trophies he found rather more than he had bargained for. A portion of torn flesh with fragments of knitted grey pullover adhering to it were hardly on young Richard's wish list and sent him running back to his nearby Parkfield Avenue home horrified and revolted by what he had seen. Twelve-year-old Lilian Ward had an equally shocking introduction to the reality of war when another young lad frightened her by gleefully showing her a severed arm. Jack Laycock was a local Observer Corps member and he, too, picked his way across the marshland the next morning to view the scene for himself. It was an awful panorama that unfolded as he approached. What he witnessed he described as being "…like the surface of the moon with mud and clods of soil as far as one could see". Nearby he saw the local newspaper photographer, Wilf Bignell, who pointed to a small pile of aeroplane pieces and, next to it, a gruesomely blood-stained hessian sack. Bignell lifted the sack and underneath it lay most of a black flying boot with a zip up one side and, shockingly, the foot and leg of the unfortunate wearer still inside. The grisly spectacle of utter carnage now unfolded to more and more sightseers, to the police and to service personnel as they all arrived on the scene that had been the aftermath of what had been a brief and violent aerial engagement which had sent this German aircraft plunging into the marsh taking its unfortunate crew with it.

As usual with events of this nature, the crash site was investigated by RAF air intelligence officers of A.I.2(g) but when they arrived at Shinewater Marsh there was very little for them to record. Often, and certainly by this stage of the war, their reports on crashed enemy aircraft ran to many pages of detail. This time just six brief lines would suffice:

> "Report 8/5 – Me 410
>
> This aircraft was shot down by a Mosquito at 22.45 hours on 8th November at Friday Street near Eastbourne. Its bomb load exploded on impact and caused a crater about 100ft in diameter to be blown in rather boggy ground. No parts of the aircraft except fragments of spars could be found outside the crater. A few bits were seen in the centre of the hole but owing to the soft nature of the ground could not be reached.
>
> H G Morison
>
> Flight Lieutenant (for Wing Commander) A.I.2(g)"

10th October, 1944.

Enemy Aircraft brought down or crash landed within the County Borough of Eastbourne.

Date	Type	Location
16.8.40	Enemy bomber	Meads District
30.9.40	M.E. 109	Langney
20.5.42	M.E. 109	Downs near Beachy Head.
26.8.42	F.W. 190	Lottbridge Drove
9.11.43	M.E. 410	Friday Street.

The first clue as to the date of the incident and the aircraft type was discovered in 1970 by the author in this brief report contained in local air raid incident records. It was a starting point that ultimately led to a trail unravelling what had become of the two-man crew of this aircraft.

Sqn Ldr W 'Bill' Maguire was the 85 Squadron Mosquito pilot who shot down the Shinewater Marsh Messerschmitt 410.

His radar operator/navigator was Fg Off W D Jones, posing here with his Mosquito at RAF West Malling.

Usually, reports of this type would comment upon the fate of the crew. Significantly in this case the report is entirely silent on the matter of the aircrew or their condition – ie POW, injured or dead. However, local information on the matter of the crew was very specific and both men had clearly perished. Aside from that sparse detail, additional information was scant indeed when the author first investigated the Shinewater Marsh incident during 1969. All that was known was that it was a Messerschmitt 410 although the first intimation of the aircraft type was when the author first researched the incident and found a one line entry in local ARP reports that listed wartime air crashes. This stated that the aircraft had been shot down on the night of 8/9 November 1943. Further delving in published sources revealed that it had been shot down by a Mosquito and that both the German crew members had died. They were, however, all useful starting points for further research, despite the paucity of detail.

In 1969/70, though, research tools by way of any published resources, for example, were scant to say the very least and access to even the National Archives (then the Public Record Office) was not exactly as simple as it is today. Research of this kind, now widely undertaken

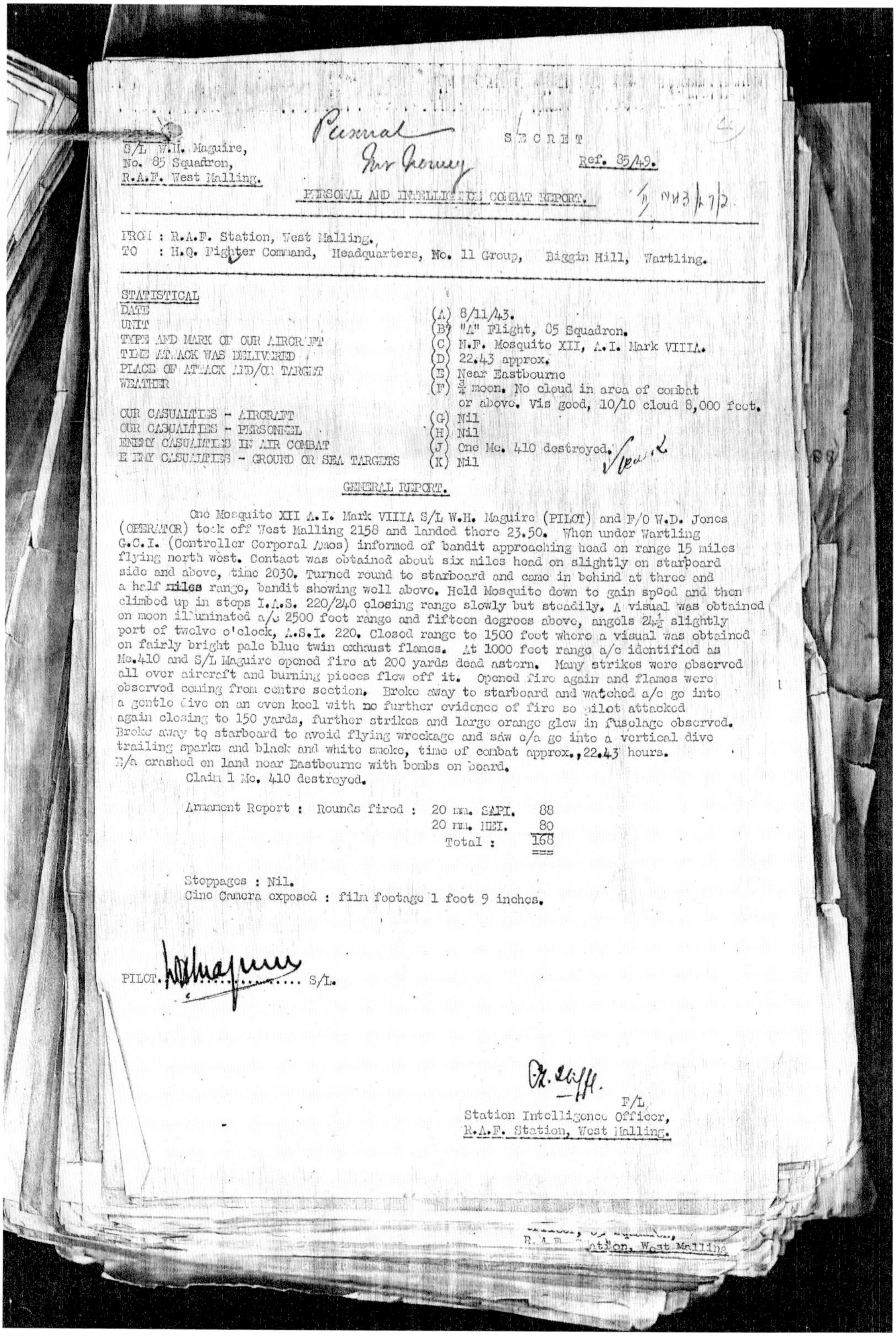

S/L W.H. Maguire,
No. 85 Squadron,
R.A.F. West Malling.

Pursual
Mr Tenney

SECRET

Ref. 85/49.

PERSONAL AND INTELLIGENCE COMBAT REPORT.

FROM : R.A.F. Station, West Malling,
TO : H.Q. Fighter Command, Headquarters, No. 11 Group, Biggin Hill, Wartling.

STATISTICAL

DATE	(A)	8/11/43.
UNIT	(B)	"A" Flight, 85 Squadron.
TYPE AND MARK OF OUR AIRCRAFT	(C)	N.F. Mosquito XII, A.I. Mark VIIIA.
TIME ATTACK WAS DELIVERED	(D)	22.43 approx.
PLACE OF ATTACK AND/OR TARGET	(E)	Near Eastbourne
WEATHER	(F)	¾ moon. No cloud in area of combat or above. Vis good, 10/10 cloud 8,000 feet.
OUR CASUALTIES - AIRCRAFT	(G)	Nil
OUR CASUALTIES - PERSONNEL	(H)	Nil
ENEMY CASUALTIES IN AIR COMBAT	(J)	One Me. 410 destroyed.
ENEMY CASUALTIES - GROUND OR SEA TARGETS	(K)	Nil

GENERAL REPORT.

One Mosquito XII A.I. Mark VIIIA S/L W.H. Maguire (PILOT) and F/O W.D. Jones (OPERATOR) took off West Malling 2158 and landed there 23.50. When under Wartling G.C.I. (Controller Corporal Amos) informed of bandit approaching head on range 15 miles flying north west. Contact was obtained about six miles head on slightly on starboard side and above, time 2030. Turned round to starboard and came in behind at three and a half miles range, bandit showing well above. Held Mosquito down to gain speed and then climbed up in steps I.A.S. 220/240 closing range slowly but steadily. A visual was obtained on moon illuminated a/c 2500 feet range and fifteen degrees above, angels 24½ slightly port of twelve o'clock, A.S.I. 220. Closed range to 1500 feet where a visual was obtained on fairly bright pale blue twin exhaust flames. At 1000 feet range a/c identified as Me.410 and S/L Maguire opened fire at 200 yards dead astern. Many strikes were observed all over aircraft and burning pieces flew off it. Opened fire again and flames were observed coming from centre section. Broke away to starboard and watched a/c go into a gentle dive on an even keel with no further evidence of fire so pilot attacked again closing to 150 yards, further strikes and large orange glow in fuselage observed. Broke away to starboard to avoid flying wreckage and saw a/c go into a vertical dive trailing sparks and black and white smoke, time of combat approx., 22.43 hours. E/a crashed on land near Eastbourne with bombs on board.

Claim 1 Me. 410 destroyed.

Armament Report : Rounds fired : 20 mm. SAPI. 88
20 mm. HEI. 80
Total : 168

Stoppages : Nil.
Cine Camera exposed : film footage 1 foot 9 inches.

PILOT. W.H. Maguire S/L.

F/L,
Station Intelligence Officer,
R.A.F. Station, West Malling.

The combat report filed by Maguire and Jones after the engagement.

by thousands and greatly aided by the internet, was in many ways in its infancy. Some might even call this particular area of historical research during the 1960s and 70s pioneering and groundbreaking work that provided a basis for much of what is known today about the 1939-45 air war over Britain. It was then a case of groping around for some more clues, often with very little idea as to where to begin the search. When those clues eventually came to light in respect of the Shinewater Messerschmitt they were in part useful and, in part, frustrating at the same time.

The first piece of the jig-saw was to establish who had shot the Me 410 down. Helpfully, the air intelligence report had confirmed the victor to have been a Mosquito and it was a relatively simple matter to establish that this was a claim of 85 Squadron based at RAF West Malling. A surviving combat report in the National Archives was specific as to the claim, giving date, time, aircraft type and location. The Mosquito had been flown by Squadron Leader W H 'Bill' Maguire DFC with his radar operator Flying Officer W D Jones. Whilst the combat report is shown in detail here, the post-war account of Fg Off Jones written in 1972 adds rather more colour to the event than does the contemporary 1943 report. Jones was tracked down by the author to the East Sussex village of Ticehurst where, in the 1970s, he was headmaster of the village primary school – just a few miles from where his Me 410 victim had fallen and also close to his wartime base in Kent.

> "I happen to have my log book and I have checked the details. We took off at 22.00hrs on the 8th in appalling weather conditions; torrential rain, cloud base practically on the ground at West Malling and on the first bounce we were airborne in cloud and came out of cloud at about 17,000ft to a cloudless full or near full moon. The light was dazzling. We were sent southwards and picked up contact when over the Channel, way above us and coming towards us. We turned and climbed, levelled off at about 25,000ft, closed in, recognised it as a 410 flying absolutely straight and level, fired, saw it go down, enter the cloud and that was that. It was probably about 22.50. We landed after some difficulty owing to cloud and poor visibility at about midnight."

Sadly, Maguire was killed in a flying accident later in the war but the detail left in his combat report, and in Jones's subsequent post-war account, is a fulsome testimony to the events relating to the downing of the Shinewater Marsh Me 410 and they supplement those who witnessed things at ground level that night. One question still remained, though. What of the Messerschmitt 410 and its crew? What was the identity of both the aeroplane and its unfortunate occupants?

In many cases of this kind local burials of German aircrew can very quickly fill in all the missing details and since it was known that both crew members had been killed it was not unreasonable to assume that they had been buried somewhere nearby. In view of the crash location within the county borough of Eastbourne, the likely place of interment was either of the town's municipal cemeteries although both drew a complete blank. No German aircrew, either identified or unknown, and who could possibly have been linked to the Shinewater incident were buried *anywhere* nearby and it very soon became clear that the

In 1970 the crater seen on page 133 was still there and had become a cattle-watering pond. Today, the pond still exists as part of Shinewater Country Park.

sad remains of the crew found at the time of the crash were probably quietly disposed of at the scene. Most likely they were simply consigned to the ever deepening water of the crater caused by the violence of a high speed impact from 25,000ft and the subsequent detonation of on-board bombs. So, the question still remained; who were these two men?

Examination of Luftwaffe reports for that night threw up three Me 410s lost on operations over England. These were:-

Me 410 A-1 (W.Nr 10311) 14/KG2, U5+HE, Fw Knie and Uffz Abel missing.
Me 410 A-1 (W.Nr 10262) 14/KG2, U5+JF, Uffz Holzmann and Uffz Fischer missing.
Me 410 A-1 (W.Nr 10244) 15/KG2, U5+BF, Hptm Schmitter and Uffz Hainzinger missing.

Additionally, it was also known that two of the three went into the sea – one downed off Clacton by 488 Squadron at midnight, the other off Beachy Head by 29 Squadron at around 10.15 but, unfortunately, identification of the Shinewater crew by a process of elimination was in effect ruled out because *all* the crews lost that night remained unaccounted for. Of the two Me 410s down in the sea, no trace of any of the four crew members had ever been found. Whilst research had drawn up a shortlist of three candidates it was still impossible to say out of those crews who had been brought down at Eastbourne by Maguire and Jones. Some further evidence was required and this was clearly only going to be obtained

Ex Fg Off Jones attended one of the 1976 site excavations and is seen here with a propeller blade from the aircraft he helped to shoot down.

through an excavation at the point of impact – this was still, in the 1970s, a water-filled crater in a grazing meadow that had now become a cattle-watering point. That said, the violence of the crash and explosion did not bode well for the possibility of any meaningful discoveries even if excavation were possible.

At that time there were no legal restrictions imposed upon the investigation and recovery of wartime aircraft wrecks in the UK. More importantly in this specific instance, of course, there were no barriers to prevent the recovery of wrecks where aircrew remained missing as in this case. Such restrictions, later imposed by the 1986 Protection of Military Remains Act, would have prevented the crash site investigations on the land at Morning's Mill Farm that got underway in the early 1970s and which were ultimately to solve the mystery of one missing Luftwaffe crew.

First, the site came under investigation by a team of air cadets led by the late Warrant Officer Ron Lockyer of 54 (Eastbourne) Squadron, Air Training Corps. Not surprisingly those efforts revealed little of any value despite an extensive grapnel hook dredge of the crater

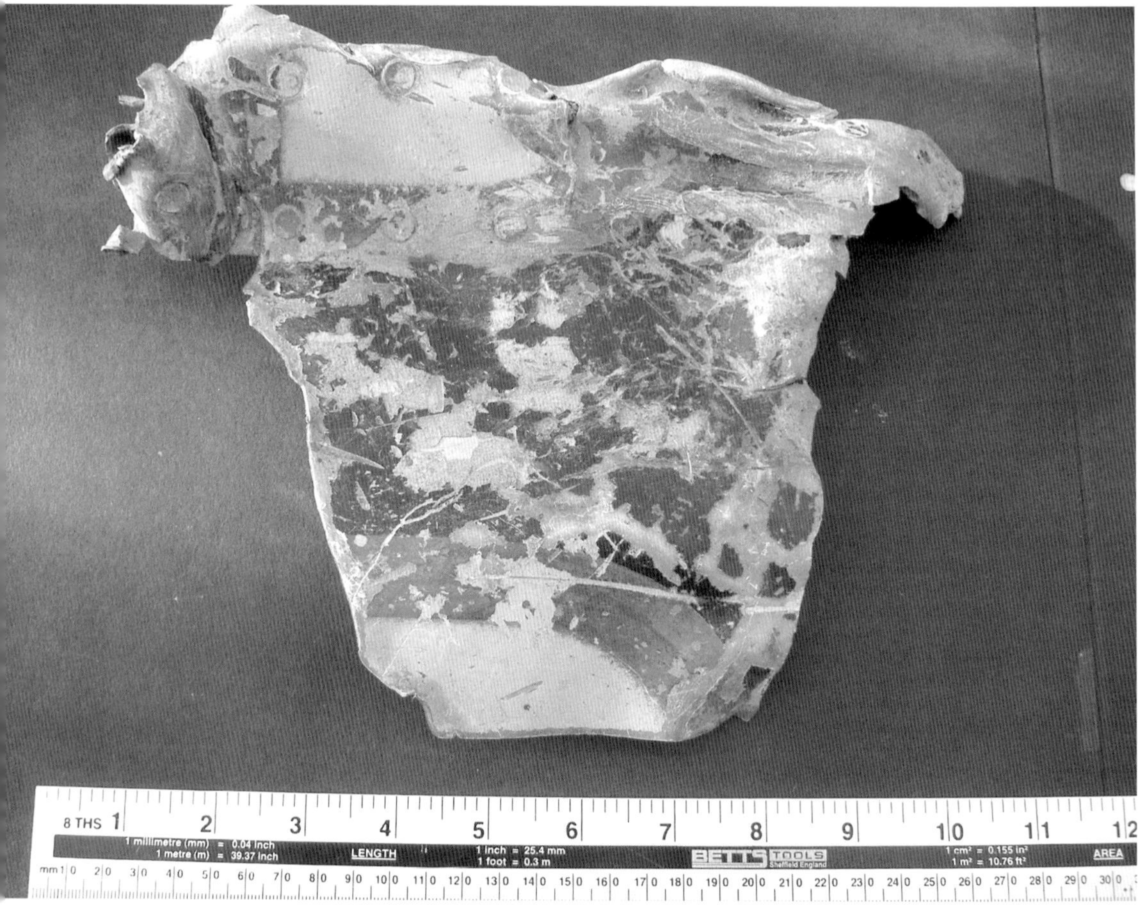

Amongst artefacts retrieved from the crater during several 1970s excavations at the site was this portion of fuselage bearing its light blue camouflage and parts of a black letter B outlined in red. This find helped point to the identify of aircraft and crew, these identities later being confirmed by the discovery of a metal tag bearing the aircraft Werke Nummer.

and a brief dive by some hardy members of the Eastbourne sub-aqua club. From the glutinous mud were trawled a few twisted airframe parts, including a portion of rear fuselage marked: 'Vor dem aufbocken mit 400 kg belasten'. Nothing else besides this came to light. Leastways, nothing that aided identification in any meaningful way. If the crater held any vital clues at all then they were clearly buried deeper. Much deeper.

By 1973 the Wealden Aviation Archaeological Group had taken matters a stage further with an attempt to excavate the periphery of the crater using a wheeled JCB. Again, little of any significance was found save for a quantity of exploded 13mm cannon shell cases and bomb shrapnel. The only other thing discovered was that the edge of the crater was perilously boggy and almost resulted in the loss of the digging machine, it almost joining the Me 410 wreck in the murky water. Any further attempt needed a tracked excavator with a further reach and so in 1976 the Wealden group returned again, this time bringing a Hymac digger to the site. In the presence of former Flying Officer W D Jones there were at last some more tangible results. A propeller blade, a drogue parachute, parts of aircraft

Hptm Wilhelm Schmitter, Staffelkapitän of 14./KG 2, was the pilot of the Messerschmitt 410 downed at Shinewater Marsh.

Uffz Felix Hainzinger was Schmitter's crewman.

weaponry, a section of aileron bearing the entry and exit hole of a 20mm shell and a whole mass of other airframe parts broke the surface.

Significant amongst these was a portion of blue-painted fuselage, distinctly bearing the remains of a black letter 'B' which was outlined in red. Of the three Messerschmitt 410s lost that night only one fitted the bill and that was the aircraft U5 + **B**F flown by Schmitter and Hainzinger. Final confirmation came with the discovery of a small alloy tag marked 10244 which was indeed the Werke Nummer of Schmitter's U5 + BF. Proof positive that the last resting place of Wilhelm Schmitter and Felix Hainzinger had finally been identified.

Although the identification was 100% certain, no trace of either man came to light and given the ferocity of the impact and explosion, and the scattered bodily remains found there in 1943, this was perhaps not surprising. The nearest tangible item associated with the men themselves was the badly shredded remnants of a drogue parachute from either the pilot's or radio operator/air gunner's main parachute packs. This had been dragged up from a depth of some six metres under the bottom of the crater. The uncertainty surrounding the demise of these two men, missing since 1943, endures to this day although the German military archive office was sufficiently satisfied by the 1976 discoveries to amend their records to show the place of death as having being confirmed at Eastbourne.

Bringing the story rather more up to date, the fields of Shinewater Marsh and what had once been a part of Morning's Mill Farm have now changed beyond any recognition from how they had been in 1943. Indeed, the area has changed today beyond any recognition from how it had appeared to the author in the 1970s. Now, a new link road slices across the marsh and industrial units have advanced towards the western side of the crash site. To the east, and out towards Langney, houses and roads have further encroached and the site itself has now been swallowed up by the 1990s development of what is now Shinewater Country Park off the newly constructed Larkspur Drive. The former Sussex wetlands have been sculpted and landscaped, planted, and in every way transformed. Huge water features have been created by the construction of flood compensation lakes and a new school, Shinewater County Secondary, has been built just yards away from where the Messerschmitt 410 crashed.

But what of the crater today? Incredibly, and amidst all the huge changes to the landscape surrounding it, the water-filled crater still exists in a completely transformed environment. Fenced off, and completely insignificant as ponds go, the 'Messerschmitt crater' is still there. Nothing today marks it out as anything out of the ordinary. No marker stone to record the passing of two young lives that were violently snuffed out there, and nothing at all to give any clues as to the dramatic events behind its creation. Visiting the site to take comparison photos in November 2008, the author was engaged in conversation by a curious walker who wanted to know why the pond was of such interest as to warrant being photographed. He had passed that way almost every day for over fifteen years and had never given the apparently insignificant patch of water a second glance or even a second thought. "I thought it was just an ordinary pond," he remarked. In fact, this is a far from ordinary pond and is in effect the grave of Hptm Schmitter and Uffz Hainzinger. However, both men are still officially missing.

CHAPTER 14

"The Dornier on my Left Exploded..."

BY 16 AUGUST 1940 the Battle of Britain was certainly upping in tempo – if not reaching some kind of imminent crescendo. This was the day that saw Dornier 17-Z pilot Lt Heinz-Georg Möllenbrok (author of the foreword to this book) shot down over Kent to be taken POW with very serious injuries. He was also witness to the destruction of another Dornier 17 from his unit flying alongside him, the loss of which gave rise to a long-running saga relating to some of its still missing crew members. That saga is still ongoing as this book goes to press, although first we need to let Möllenbrok take us back to 16 August 1940:

"It was my seventh raid on England with KG 2, although the commander of the Gruppe was troubled that he had to continue sending his young crews over England knowing that many would be shot down.

"I had been involved in the raid on Eastchurch on 13 August 1940 when we were without our fighter escort because we didn't receive the radio signal that had cancelled the raid. So far, apart from Eastchurch, we had attacked Manston twice, Lympne and Hawkinge as well as shipping in the Channel although I don't think we did much damage to the vessels we attacked.

"On 16 August we were flying from our base at Cambrai and our target was to be Hornchurch, although when we reached the Thames Estuary around 15.45 hours we found the London area was all shrouded in fog and the cloud base was at 3,000ft although we had been promised clear weather in the late afternoon. As we were still under the instruction only to bomb military targets, and when we found we could not attack our target, we ditched our bombs over the Thames and our twenty-seven Dorniers all turned for home. As we were turning, dropping our bombs and heading for France we were suddenly attacked by Hurricanes and the Dornier on my left exploded. We feared all the crew must be dead. We tried to keep formation because we all had our ground-attack 20mm cannons and could fire on any fighters from the front or below – but the Hurricanes came from the rear and above. Four Hurricanes attacked our section and the starboard engine was hit on my Dornier and although I tried to hold the machine on one engine we started to loose formation. Later, when we had dropped out of formation and

Lt Heinz Möllenbrok was pilot of a 3./KG 2 Dornier 17-Z shot down over east Kent on 16 August 1940. His comrades in another 3./KG 2 machine shot down in the same action were all killed and are linked to the mystery burials of 'unknown' German airmen at Whitstable. Here, Möllenbrok is at the controls of a He 111 although he was shot down in a Dornier 17. With him is Uffz Gordon Gollob, killed in the 16 August incident.

were alone, the steering mechanism was hit making the bomber difficult to control and I found myself flying over Canterbury. In the final attack, which was near Eastry, we were sent spinning down and on fire. The hatch was below the cockpit, and both the observer and I tried to exit at the same time and because of the spinning motion of the aircraft we became wedged against the fuselage sides. One of the other two crew members knocked out the glazed panel above the cockpit and both of them exited that way. I am sure they must have hit some part of the aircraft and both were almost surely dead before they struck the ground.

"The first thing I can remember after baling out was hanging from my parachute straps in a tree and seeing the barrel of a shotgun being pointed up at me. I couldn't see much as I came down because it was misty but I thought how the farms with their little fields and meadows looked just like the countryside at my home in Schleswig Holstein. Two men, whom I now know were Ron Crier and Tony Wanstall, tried to get me down from my harness. They twisted the release box and gave it a good whack. I couldn't help

When this Dornier 17-Z of 8./KG 2 was shot down onto the mudflats at Seasalter, Kent, on 13 August 1940, three of the four crew were killed. They are also linked to the conundrum of the 'unknown' German burials in Whitstable cemetery.

> myself as my right arm was badly injured and was hanging from just a strip of flesh and the bone was completely smashed and broken from hitting something when I had left the aircraft. The two men helped me to a sofa in a farmhouse, but as I was bleeding so much and didn't want to spoil the lady's furniture I asked for a chair. The lady had been a VAD nurse in the first war, and was so kind, gentle and quiet as she patched me up before I was taken off to hospital. I think someone also gave me a drop of whisky, too."

Together with his fellow crew member, Uffz Hess, Möllenbrok had had a very lucky escape indeed unlike his colleagues in the Dornier which had been seen to blow up in the air alongside them. (Author's Note: The third Dornier 17-Z flying in the 3rd Staffel Kette with Möllenbrok and Brandenburg was being flown by Ofw Hans Gerlach. His aircraft was hit and badly damaged but he struggled back to Calais where Gerlach and his crew all baled out.) It is in part the story of the Dornier that Möllenbrok saw go down, and its crew, which is intertwined with what can only be described as a puzzle involving other crew members from Dornier 17s of KG 2 lost during the 13 August raid on Eastchurch, and in which Möllenbrok had also participated. As we shall see, it is indeed a convoluted tale.

When the Dornier formation was attacked it was with such suddenness and ferocity that one of the aircraft, the one whose destruction was witnessed by Möllenbrok, had no time to ditch its bomb load. Hit by a fusillade of .303 bullets from close-quarters the Dornier erupted into a fireball and fell onto the foreshore at Whitstable. The attacker had been Flt Sgt F W 'Taffy' Higginson:

> "I was Green 1 in the squadron formation. I was told to take my section and attack the fighters. My section climbed but were getting left behind. I then saw a Dornier 17 break away from the formation and closed to about 300 yards. I gave a burst of about two seconds. He then dived through the clouds and I followed him down and attacked from the quarter. I then made another attack from astern and observed the enemy aircraft burning in the fuselage behind the main planes. I gave a quick burst and the enemy aircraft crashed on the beach near Whitstable and burst into flames. I took cine pictures of him blazing to complete my film, but just then my aircraft burst into flames and I made an emergency landing south of Whitstable. I was picked up by the London Irish Rifles who witnessed the attack and confirm my enemy aircraft crashing and bursting into flames. I must have been hit in the engine, though I did not observe the return fire from the enemy aircraft. I was unhurt. My film was destroyed.
>
> F W Higginson – Flt Sgt"

As Möllenbrok and his crew had concluded there had been no survivors following Higginson's attack and the blazing aircraft broke up on impact with the beach. Later, there was also an explosion although it is not clear whether this was fuel or one or more bombs from its weapon load detonating. Whatever, the fierce fighter attack and subsequent fireball, a high velocity impact with the beach and then a violent explosion literally tore apart the aircraft and its unfortunate crew of whom, sadly, there was very little left to find or to bury. That said, and although they could not be identified at the time, they were duly buried with full military honours at Whitstable's Millstrood Road Cemetery. The interment was in a single coffin in what was designated 'War Grave 1', the burial taking place just the day after they had been killed in action.

It was, perhaps, an extraordinarily rapid turn of events to see them buried so quickly but things were almost certainly expedited with such unusual rapidity because two other unidentified airmen who had been killed on 13 August at nearby Seasalter were due for burial at Whitstable on the 17th and with the graves prepared and funeral arrangements already having been made for those casualties. Clearly, it made sense to the authorities to deal with all the burials at once, and the graves for the two 13 August casualties were simply given extra depth so as to enable the coffin containing the four casualties from the 16 August incident to be buried on top of them. As for the two Luftwaffe airmen killed in the Seasalter crash, both had defied formal identification by the British authorities although an identity disc was found for each man, one marked 69 446/4 and the other 69 644/37. Although in 1940 these numbers did not help identify them to the burial authority they would, much later, become crucial in the whole Whitstable Dornier jigsaw.

As for the 13 August 1940 losses suffered by KG 2, these no doubt helped cement the view of the III./KG 2 commander who had evidently expressed reservations about sending his young men out to die in raids that experience had already shown would likely be very costly in terms of his unit's casualty rate. As we have seen, the events this day had conspired against the Dorniers of KG 2 from the very outset when wireless messages ordering a recall were not received and the bombers continued to their target without a fighter escort. In all, some five Dorniers from different elements of KG 2 were shot down and another seven returned to France damaged and with a number of crew members wounded. KG 2 had paid a heavy price and one of the losses, a Dornier from 7./KG 2, had seen three of its crew killed and the fourth captured when it smashed itself to destruction on the mudflats off Seasalter. When investigators picked their way across the glutinous mud of The Oaze they found two of the crew smashed beyond recognition in the crumpled bomber. These were the two men buried at Whitstable on 17 August with only their identity disc numbers recorded.

Of the other two on board, one of them (Fw Rudolf Haensgen) was wounded and taken prisoner and the other (Ofw Karl Langer) was washed ashore at nearby Graveney Marshes and buried in Graveney Churchyard on 22 August 1940. The other two crew members who had been killed, Oblt Walter Morich and Oblt Gerhard Müller, had both baled out too low and died when their parachutes failed to open. Of these latter two, it is highly likely that an unidentified body washed ashore sometime later and buried as an unknown German airman at Whitstable on 20 August was Oblt Morich. As to Müller it is now possible to identify him from one of the identity disc numbers (69 646/4) recorded against one of the Whitstable burials from 17 August. To complicate matters further, another KG 2 Dornier crewman from another aircraft lost on 13 August was also washed up and found at Whitstable around the same time, and from his identity number (69 644/37) we can identify him as Oblt Horst von der Groeben. He was the other man buried with Müller. If the story is not already convoluted and complicated enough it gets yet more curious!

When in October 1962 the German War Graves Service exhumed the graves at Whitstable for re-interment at Cannock Chase German Military Cemetery it appeared, at least initially, that all of the German burials at Millstrood Road Cemetery had been removed. And yet there was a problem. Given that the two unknown airmen buried beneath the remains of the four Dornier crew members out of the 16 August Whitstable crash had both been buried with identity numbers registered, then one would have certainly expected that upon exhumation names would have been duly matched against these service numbers and, as a result, the graves of Oblt Müller and Oblt von der Groeben would now appear at Cannock. However, they do not appear there. Not only that, but there are no graves of two unknown airmen at Cannock that might be matched to the Whitstable pair. Somewhere, and somehow, something had gone awry and both men currently remain missing – notwithstanding that two burials are recorded at Whitstable against which these two Luftwaffe officer's service numbers are logged. The explanation behind this rather bizarre and macabre mystery is relatively simple and in recent years it has emerged that, due to an inexplicable mistake, and when the remains of the four 16 August casualties were exhumed from War Grave Number 1, the exhumation team did not realise that the graves of another two men lay underneath them. Consequently, they have remained forgotten and (officially) unidentified. Both the German War Graves Service and Whitstable Cemetery had previously been unaware that the two men were still there.

Since 2005 there have been moves to have the matter rectified and in an extraordinarily complex case the German War Graves Service, Commonwealth War Graves Commission, Canterbury City Council, Home Office, Diocese of Canterbury and next-of-kin have all been involved. The aim, ultimately, is to have the remains exhumed, formally identified, and re-buried at Cannock Chase and in November 2005 Lord Falconer, then Secretary of State at the Home Office, duly signed licences for the exhumations of Gerhard Müller and Horst von der Groeben from Whitstable. Mired in red tape and formalities, these exhumations have not yet been carried out and the licences signed by Lord Falconer have now expired. However, and as this book was going to print, further moves by the German War Graves Service were understood to be imminent in order to draw together all the strands in the case and bring about some conclusion.

Quite possibly some may think that this is an awful lot of fuss over two long-dead German airmen, although it is worth reflecting upon the pronouncements of Judge Richard Walker (for the commissary general of the City & Diocese of Canterbury) when, *inter alia*, he quoted Bishop Hill of Stafford:

> "The permanent burial of the physical body should be seen as a symbol of our entrusting the person to God for resurrection. We are commending the person to God, saying farewell to them for their journey and entrusting them in peace for their ultimate destination."

Of course, it might reasonably be argued that the criteria Bishop Hill set out had already been met by the interments on 17 August 1940 when both men were given Christian burials in consecrated ground. If this is accepted as a given, then letting the two men rest in peace where they were originally buried might seem the most appropriate course of action. All that might then be needed is the erection of German War Graves Service headstones at Whitstable naming the two men. Unfortunately, it is not as simple as that since the German authorities are now requiring proof that the remains are actually there (ie *sight* of them) before erecting headstones. Under the circumstances their preferred course of action would be the removal of the two men to Cannock, and in the case of at least one of the two sets of relatives involved it is understood that they concur with this view.

For the time being at least these two lost fliers from the Battle of Britain remain in something of a limbo; whilst it is certain where they are buried and who they are their graves are unmarked and they continue to be regarded as officially missing in action.

CHAPTER 15 No Longer Unknown

Ofw Leo Raida, crew member of a Messerschmitt 410 downed off Felixstowe on the night of 13/14 July 1943.

WHEN JOE POTTER PAID visits to tend his mother's grave in Felixstowe Cemetery during the 1990s the ex-serviceman could not help but be intrigued by the grave to an unknown German airman in the cemetery's war graves plot. It stood next to the grave of another German flier, Fw Franz Zwissler, and when Joe made enquiries with the cemetery superintendent he was surprised to be told that a service number actually existed in the burial register for this airman. As an ex-serviceman, Joe realised at once that if an identity disc number was known for this man then it must surely be possible to put a name to that number. After all, that was the whole purpose of a serviceman's number and identity disc. To Joe it begged a very simple question; how on earth could this man be unknown? It was a mystery that he resolved to unravel and it set him upon a path that ultimately would see no less than nineteen individual Luftwaffe airmen identified and named who had previously been buried in the UK as unknown. In short, it became a one-man campaign to identify the Luftwaffe fallen within the British Isles and, more recently, in France as well.

The Lowestoft case, Joe's first, was to be a relatively steep learning curve for him. He was a novice at this kind of research and, at first, he had to very much find his way in the research maze and discover who-was-who in various organisations such as the Commonwealth and German war graves services. However, the man buried next to Franz Zwissler was a relatively easy nut to crack. First, since his date of burial matched that of Zwissler it was not unreasonable to assume that this man might well have been linked to that casualty through being a fellow crew member and indeed that proved to be the case. With the service number recorded in the Felixstowe burial register it was a relatively simple matter to check the German loss returns for Zwissler, a Messerschmitt 410 pilot of 16./KG 2 downed on the night of 13/14 July 1943. Recorded on the loss return was the name of his crew member Ofw Leo Raida, and against that name the very same service number that was recorded in the register. Case proven! But what of the background as to how these two men came to be buried in Lowestoft?

Researcher Joe Potter managed to establish that an unknown German airman buried in Lowestoft was in fact Leo Raida.

The Messerschmitt 410 was a new weapon on the Luftwaffe inventory when it came into front-line operational use during the early summer of 1943 and was operated by the V./KG 2 as night bomber/intruders but it was not until the night of 13/14 July that the type was first encountered by RAF night-fighter aircraft. On that night a Mosquito of 85 Squadron, based at RAF Hunsdon and flown by Flt Lt E N Bunting and Plt Off F French, had encountered radar contacts on 'bogey' aircraft approaching the British coast. Two contacts were made, but Bunting turned onto the second of the pair and eventually spotted visually pairs of exhaust flames at 7,000ft range. Climbing at full speed and maximum boost the Mosquito very slowly gained ground on the fast moving and climbing aircraft. As they climbed, in hot pursuit, so the Rolls-Royce Merlin engines on the Mosquito began to overheat chasing this fast aeroplane and required some judicious juggling of radiator flaps and throttles in the chase which went on for some fifteen minutes.

Eventually, at 25,000 ft, the range had closed sufficiently to allow the two Mosquito crew to get a visual contact on their quarry although what they saw puzzled them. It wasn't one of the usual German types and its similarity to a Mosquito was uncanny. Finally, after some deliberation, the pair convinced themselves that the exhaust configuration and its bright blue exhaust flames were clearly distinguishable from a Mosquito and closed in for the kill. Buffeted by the slipstream, the unseen Mosquito blasted the enemy aircraft with two short bursts of one hundred and twenty rounds of 20mm cannon shells. Instantly, the German machine caught fire, rolled onto its back and dived vertically into the sea off Felixstowe at around 12.10 hours. The first Messerschmitt 410 had been lost to British defences and it had taken with it into the North Sea its two crew, Franz Zwissler and Leo Raida.

During the course of his research into the unknown Felixstowe casualty Joe Potter's investigative trail had led to him initially seeking assistance from the German chancellor, Helmut Kohl, after which his correspondence was directed to various channels in Germany and, finally, to him receiving confirmation from the German War Graves Service that the evidence of identification had been accepted by the German authorities and that a replacement headstone, bearing Raida's name, would be erected over the grave. To Joe, this was both a triumph and a vindication of his view that this unknown man could and should be identified and named. However, he remained initially concerned as to how any such news reaching the Raida family in Germany might be received. Would this be seen as opening up old wounds from Germany's dark and recent past? Or would it be viewed positively and welcomed by a family who had long wondered what had happened to a loved one? There was only one way to find out, and Joe set out with considerable trepidation to compose what he described as "...the hardest letter I have ever had to write", addressing it to Frau Erika Kryczun, the widow of Leo Raida. What came back utterly overwhelmed him.

Frau Kryczun was "moved to tears" by the discovery of where her late husband lay, and the case had a special poignancy, too, for other reasons. First, it transpired that Zwissler and Raida had been close friends, even pre-war, and it seemed appropriate that it could now be recognised that the two pals lay side-by-side. Additionally, when Leo was posted missing Erika Raida was pregnant with their first child – although neither she nor Leo had been aware that they were expectant parents before he was lost. Sadly, their only son was later to die through illness during his forties and Erika subsequently decided that the memorial lantern from her son's grave should be moved to Leo's grave making a touching link between father and son – a son who never knew his father and vice-versa. When, in August 1997, the new headstone was finally dedicated at Felixstowe it had made up Joe Potter's mind. As Heinz Möllenbrok laid a wreath on Leo Raida's grave on behalf of the old comrades of KG 2, Joe decided he would expand his quest for other unknown German airmen buried in the UK who might yet be identifiable. To all intents and purposes, the Felixstowe case had really been accidental. Joe now decided to move into a more pro-active hunt.

Over a period of nearly fifteen years he has sought out the unknown German burials at Cannock and elsewhere in the British Isles and carefully re-examined the paper trails that invariably lead from the recording of the crash itself, to the original burials, through exhumations for removal to Cannock and the Cannock burial registers themselves. Very often the clues are tortuous and sometimes tenuous. Other times, as in the Raida case, they are clear and indisputable. However, to Joe Potter each pursuit of sometimes elusive facts

Lt Günther Beubler was a crew man from a Junkers 188 shot down near the Spurn lighthouse on the night of 2/3 October 1943. Originally, he was buried at Hull as an unknown German airman.

has but one goal in sight – to see another name ticked off the missing list and yet another family told where their kin lies buried. Overall, and at the time this book was in preparation, nearly twenty names have been added (at least nominally) to headstones previously inscribed 'unknown' through Potter's indefatigable and tireless efforts. Whilst some of the cases are far too complex to cover in any detail here, or at least do full justice to Joe's work, a list of all his proven cases is appended to this chapter. However, one case that was possibly the simplest of them all was that of two Germans buried as unknown in Hull (Northern) Cemetery.

Incredibly, when he checked the burial register for details of these two men he found their names already recorded there; Lt Günther Beubler and Uffz Albert Fischer. And yet above their graves stood two headstones describing the occupants as unknown. Somehow there had been a failure along the way to record the names on the original grave markers. Leastways, it seems that nobody had ever bothered to check and that situation had remained unchanged since 1943. Beubler and Fischer must have been the two easiest and most obvious cases to solve, since the answer as to who they were had been there all along. Both men had died on the night of 2/3 October 1943 when their Ju 188 E-1 of 2./KG 66 crashed whilst taking evasive action and had fallen onto a mud bank about half a mile from Spurn lighthouse killing all four crew. Incredibly, Beubler's centenarian mother was still living at the time his grave location was discovered making especially significant its identification and giving a great deal of comfort to a still grieving mother in her last days.

Perhaps, in view of the apparent simplicity of some of these cases, some might ask why no official efforts have ever been made to clarify who these unknown men are? The answer is simple. The German War Graves Service, now hard pressed to deal with discoveries, unmarked burials and derelict cemeteries coming to light in Poland, the former Soviet Union

Buried with him was colleague Uff Albert Fischer, also 'unknown'. Incredibly, the names of both men had been recorded in the burial register in 1943 but the names not recorded on the headstones. The case of Beubler and Fischer was another resolved by Joe Potter.

and other Eastern Bloc countries, have precious little in the way of manpower or fiscal resources to deal with such cases on a pro-active basis. Dealing with them on a reactive basis is a struggle enough. It is also important to realise that the German War Graves Service is funded entirely differently to the Commonwealth War Graves Commission. The latter is fully funded through the governments of its various member countries on a proportional basis; ie the cost of the commission's work is borne inter-governmentally in proportion to the number of war graves that each member nation has. In respect of the German War Graves Service, however, the situation is much different and the organisation is run very much on a charitable basis – much like our own RNLI, for example.

Consequently, funding is both stretched and limited and it is for this reason that of the nineteen graves identified by name through Joe Potter's work only two named headstones have thus far been erected; that for Leo Raida and also for another Messerschmitt 410 crew member, St Fw Otto Runge who had been lost on 22 January 1944, at Folkestone (New) Cemetery. Whilst the newly identified grave locations have been recorded in logs and registers, and listed on line, the headstones for the majority have been ordered but not yet engraved or erected. Another case that Joe has worked on, and solved, is the mysterious grave at Folkestone (New) Cemetery that is simply marked with a headstone engraved with the name A Schenck.

Hptm Wilhelm Enßlen had taken part in the Spanish Civil War as a fighter pilot and was one of only twenty-eight men awarded the Spanish Cross in Gold with Swords and Diamonds. An experienced fighter leader, the twenty-nine-year-old flier had taken part in the campaigns in Poland and France and had seen the Battle of Britain through, steadily adding to his score of claims. On 2 November 1940, however, he tangled in combat with a Spitfire flown by Sqn Ldr J A 'Johnny' Kent, the Canadian CO of 92 Squadron. Kent describes the combat in graphic detail in his biography *One Of The Few*:

"…The rest of the formation dived for the coast and did not attempt to turn and fight, at least all but one. We chased after the fleeing Germans and I caught up with this one and attacked. I found that I had picked an old hand; instead of just running away he waited until I was very close and then suddenly broke to the right and into the sun. I momentarily lost sight of him but as he continued to turn he moved out of the glare of the sun and a tail chase developed. As we came round full circle he repeated his manoeuvre but this time I pulled my sights through him and, although losing him under the nose of my aircraft, gave a short burst in the hopes that I might get some tracer near enough to him to frighten him into running for home. I misjudged my man, however, and he continued his tactics and apparently had no intention of running at all but finally after the fourth or fifth circle I drew my sights through him again, gave a longish burst and was startled when he suddenly appeared from under my nose and we very nearly collided. I still have a very vivid mental picture of him looking up at me as we flashed past not twenty feet apart. I distinctly remember that he had his goggles up on his helmet and his oxygen mask in place.

StFw Otto Runge was another Me 410 crew man who had been buried as unknown, this time at Folkestone. By simply associating this burial with that of his crew-mate it was possible to identify formally the unknown burial as Runge and organise a replacement headstone appropriately engraved with his name.

"I also recall the gashes along the side of the Messerschmitt where my bullets had struck and the tail of the aircraft with practically no fabric left on it and a control cable streaming back with a small piece of metal whirling around on the end of it. It is one of those pictures of a split-second's action that remains indelibly imprinted on one's mind. I did not, in the heat of the moment, fully appreciate the significance of all this and was jubilant when I saw that my opponent was reversing his turn, a fatal move in a fight, and gave him one last burst from 'fine quarter' into his left side. A thin trail of grey smoke appeared and the aircraft rolled quite slowly onto its back and started down. I immediately thought that he was getting away and followed him with throttle wide open hoping to catch him as he levelled out.

"The last time I glanced at the airspeed indicator it was registering something like 450mph but still the Me 109 outdistanced me and I finally lost it against the ground. While continuing my dive and waiting to see the grey plan-form of it as it pulled out, I

This headstone in Folkestone (New) Cemetery, Hawkinge, is inscribed with the name A Schenck. In fact, research has now established that this is the grave of Hptm Wilhelm Enßlenn of Stab.II./JG 52 shot down and killed in his Messerschmitt 109 on 2 November 1940. His identity has been confirmed by the German authorities.

was startled to see a vivid red flash and a great cloud of jet black smoke appear as the machine hit the ground and exploded.

"I came down low to see where the aircraft had struck but could see no sign of it, until I noticed some soldiers running across the fields waving to me. Then I saw it. A gaping hole that looked just like a bomb crater and hundreds of little bits scattered around.

"A few days later the Intelligence Officer told me that the pilot had been quite a highly decorated major (sic) but it had not been possible to establish his identity. Apparently I had shot away his controls and he was on the point of baling out when my last burst killed him. This was deduced from the fact that his fighting harness was picked up undone and undamaged and the left half of his tunic was found with six bullet holes in it."

In his extraordinarily detailed account of this aerial duel, Kent is absolutely correct when he says that he must have picked on "an old hand", and he is equally correct when he explains that the pilot was highly decorated although it had not been possible to establish his identity. In fact, and although he hadn't witnessed what had happened when the aircraft disappeared against the countryside below, Wilhelm Enßlenn had apparently abandoned his Messerschmitt and seemingly fallen with an unopened parachute or had somehow dropped out of his harness. Quite what happened is unclear, although it is known that he fell into the sea just beyond the low water mark at Dymchurch. According to mortuary records he was "rescued" from the sea, which rather implies that he was pulled out alive and died later. However, it seems more likely that he fell dead without an open parachute. What is not debatable, however, is that for some unknown reason his body defied identification and he was ultimately buried at Folkestone (New) Cemetery in Hawkinge under the name A Schenck.

Hptm Wilhelm Enßlenn photographed with his wife on their wedding day.

Quite where this name comes from is a mystery, although it is entirely possible that it was a tailor's name or some-such in a piece of clothing, or maybe the name of a previous owner or even a manufacturer on his parachute harness for example. Either way, no identity disc was discovered and although personal effects were found they clearly did not help put a name to the man. A piece of linking evidence, however, was found when enthusiast Steve Vizard excavated the wreck of a Messerschmitt 109 in 1982 at Hagueland, Burmarsh, just a few yards from the Romney, Hythe & Dymchurch Railway track. (Coincidentally, this was just a few fields away from the crash site of Lt Werner Knittel's Messerschmitt which is dealt with in Chapter One.) With the knowledge from RAF air intelligence reports that this crash had happened on 2 November 1940, and the fact that the unknown German airman pulled out of the sea just a short distance away had fallen from this aircraft, the discovery of the main aircraft data plate showing it to be a Messerschmitt 109 E-4 with the Werke Nummer 3784 confirmed this to indeed be the aircraft being flown by Hptm Enßlenn when he was lost. Whilst circumstantial only, and providing insufficient proof that A Schenck was indeed Wilhelm Enßlenn, it was nonetheless a most valuable piece of the jigsaw.

Once more, Joe Potter assembled all those pieces of the puzzle and presented his case to the German War Graves Service and was delighted to discover later that his evidence had been accepted. Whilst the headstone is awaiting replacement at time of this book going to print it has at least been officially confirmed that this is indeed Enßlenn's grave. His elderly widow, left wondering for nearly seventy years as to what had happened to her man, is content that in her last years she finally knows.

Thus far, the work carried out by researcher Joe Potter has led to the following positive identifications:

Lt Günther Beubler 2./KG 66 2 October 1943	Hull (Northern) Cemetery	Identified by name in burial register
Uffz Friedrich Bucholz 3./KFG 106 5 August 1942	Cannock Chase	Identified by aircraft code letters found in maintenance record book in wreckage.
Uffz Erich Clauser 9./JG 27 20 September 1940	Cannock Chase	Identified by elimination process
Ogfr Eduard Commes 3./KFG 106 5 August 1942	Cannock Chase	Identified by aircraft code letters found in maintenance record book in wreckage.
Hptm Wilhelm Ensßlen Stab II./JG 52 2 Nov 1940	Folkestone (New) Cemetery	Identified by mortuary and funeral director's records
Uffz Albert Fischer 2./KG 66 2 October 1943	Hull (Northern) Cemetery	Identified by name in burial register
Hptm Kurt Geisler 3./SKG 10 6 September 1943	Cannock Chase	Elimination through pilot's age
Gefr Karl Holzapfel 7./JG 26 6 September 1940	Folkestone (New) Cemetery	Identified by elimination process
Fw Martin Jackel 15.(Z)/LG 1 1 September 1940	Cannock Chase	Identified by elimination process
Uffz Adolf Jaggy 3./KFG 106 5 August 1942	Cannock Chase	Identified by aircraft code letters found in maintenance record book in wreckage.
Uffz Rudolf Marchlowitz 8./KG 30 5 July 1940	Folkestone (New) Cemetery	Identified from mortuary records
Uffz Amulf Neumeyer 4./KG 30 15 August 1940	Cannock Chase	Identified by elimination process
Ofw Leo Raida 16./KG 2 14 July 1943	Felixstowe	Identified by number in burial register
Fl Heinz Rösler 15.(Z)/LG 1 1 September 1940	Cannock Chase	Identified by elimination process
St Fw Otto Runge V./KG 2 22 January 1944	Folkestone (New) Cemetery	Identified by association with known and named pilot buried in adjacently numbered grave.
Gefr Günther Sobotta 3./KFG 106 5 August 1942	Cannock Chase	Identified by aircraft code letters found in maintenance record book in wreckage.
Ofw Arthur Trutwin 5./JG 53 13 August 1940	Ashes scattered Weymouth	Identified in cremation records
Fahr Erich Vortbach 1./JG 51 14 November 1940	Cannock Chase	Identified by elimination process
Oblt Heinz Weber 2./KFG 506 10 November 1941	Thornaby-on-Tees	Identified by burial slip held by the RAF Air Historical Branch.

This list of nineteen Luftwaffe personnel are those where Joe Potter's research has led to official confirmation and acceptance as to the burial location of the casualty concerned. Without this valuable independent work then these men would doubtless remain missing with unknown graves and it is important to understand that, post-war, and unlike the Allies, there was no organisation dealing with the identification and burial of German war dead. Thus, the small but important input to identification that is detailed within this book is doubly important. At the time of writing the specific work undertaken by Joe Potter remains ongoing with at least three open and still pending cases.

CHAPTER 16 One Man is Unaccounted For...

THE POLICEMAN WHO HAD been on beat duty around The Pantiles area of Tunbridge Wells on the night of 24 February 1944 was exhausted. Although it hadn't been a particularly challenging shift thus far, with perhaps the odd blackout infringement to deal with or else encouraging the odd rowdy serviceman with too much drink inside him to make it back to his billet quietly, he had played an energetic game of football that day and was shattered. Creeping into a secluded shop doorway, ostensibly to check that the door was locked, he huddled into the corner and settled down for a quick nap – bundled against the cold by his cape. In the distance he had been vaguely aware of the sound of aero engines and gunfire, but was then startled awake by the sound of a shuffling noise coming down the street towards him.

Pulling himself together he peered out into the darkness, only to be confronted by a German airman walking towards him in flying boots, overalls and full kit. At once, the airman threw up his hands and the astonished but still sleepy constable marched his unexpected prisoner to the nearest police box. Picking up the phone which had its direct line to the police station, all he could hear was the sound of a game of darts in progress in the control room! The operators were ignoring the flashing indicator lights, and with one hand gripping the German the policeman was forced to shout and bellow into the telephone to attract attention on the open line at the other end. Quite possibly the bemused German might have wondered at this point about the efficiency of British telephones, although as the airman reached inside his pockets to check their contents the policeman had a start. Was he going for a weapon?

Still nobody answered his calls, but the now smiling German offered his captor a slip of paper he had pulled out. Taking it, the policeman saw that it was a theatre ticket for a Berlin show a few days hence, the German indicating that he wouldn't now be requiring it. The frustrated officer considered his souvenir for a moment before slipping it into his pocket. Although the war was clearly drawing towards its close the prospects of making it to that particular show seemed remote to say the very least. Although at this rate, he thought, the war could well be over before anyone came to his assistance. Eventually, the flashing indicator was noticed by the control room operators and a car was duly dispatched to bring in the prisoner and red-faced constable. This somewhat surreal piece of drama with its element of farcical humour rather belied a grimmer story behind the unexpected arrival of this German airman on the streets of Tunbridge Wells, though.

During the autumn of 1943 the Luftwaffe had introduced to service its new long-range heavy bomber, the Heinkel He 177 'Greif' (Griffon), a revolutionary new design incorporating four engines albeit that these were coupled into two pairs of twin engines. With its crew of six, long operational range and heavy bomb capacity the He 177 was being employed in raids against Britain by early 1944 in Operation Steinbock. On the night of 24/25 February no less than one hundred and seventy bombers made for London, six of them heavily laden He 177 A-3s from I./KG 100. It was one of these aircraft (from the 3rd Staffel) that was to fall victim to a Mosquito of 488 Squadron flown by Flt Lt P F L Hall with his navigator Fg Off R D Marriott, the pair sending the bomber flaming into the ground at Lamberhurst on the Kent and East Sussex border.

When it struck the ground at Chequers Farm the wreckage blasted a huge crater. Of the crew of six, five had jumped from the doomed aircraft although of these only two were uninjured. One man fell without a parachute, another was injured and two were found

This was the crater blasted by the crashing He 177 at Lamberhurst, Kent, on the night of 24 February 1944. Much of the wreckage lies buried in the crater along with one of the crew members who is still posted as missing. The crater has since been filled in and levelled and is now part of Lamberhurst golf course.

dead. Of the sixth man there was no trace and it was concluded that he must be in the deeply buried wreckage of the huge bomber. With the crater later filled in, the slight dip in the corner of what had been a hop garden at Chequers Farm was finally lost to sight during the post-war development of the immediate area in the 1960s with the extension of the adjacent Lamberhurst Golf Club. Whatever was left of the Heinkel and its unfortunate occupant had apparently been lost forever under the greens of the golf course. At least, it appeared to have been lost forever.

Researcher Philippa Hodgkiss had long been fascinated by the story behind the loss of this aircraft and during April 1984 had secured permission for a non-invasive survey of the site. Her aim was to pinpoint exactly where the impact had been and to photograph the site as it then was for historical record. Ultimately, however, Philippa's quest came to naught during the 1980s with other commitments getting in the way of a long trek from her home in Abergavenny. By early 2003, however, interest in the site had come back to the top of her research agenda with knowledge that a planned by-pass for the A21 road through Lamberhurst was likely to cut across (or very close to) the crash site. Since she was aware of the approximate location of the crash, and that one man out of its crew was still unaccounted for, she felt that another approach to the club was in order. After all, she reasoned that the road builders might be blissfully unaware of what could lay in their path. Not only might they be surprised to meet a mass of buried metal in any earth-moving operations but it remained a distinct possibility that unexploded bombs might be present, too. Quite apart from the likelihood of human remains being buried there it was clearly in everyone's interests that the matter be brought to the fore again. The Middlesbrough Dornier 217 discovery had already shown that accidental discoveries were likely to occur as the increased development of hitherto inaccessible sites continued apace across the length and breadth of Britain into the twenty-first century. Against this background, then, the golf club welcomed Philippa and her team of investigators to the club to carry out their surveys.

Since the photographs of the crash site had been taken in February 1944 the landscape had understandably changed enormously, with only the remnants of an old hedge that could be seen in those photographs still in evidence at the edge of the course. It wasn't much to go on, although the golf club were aware of "an oily wet spot" that might be promising. However, with relatively meagre information the team carried out a detailed search of the area and almost immediately picked up significant readings of buried steel in one area that approximated to where the bomber was believed to have crashed. The readings were such that they left the team in no doubt that they were standing above the buried wreckage, right by the tenth and eleventh tees. As things turned out this was not, after all, an area likely to be disturbed by the impending construction of the new A 21 by-pass although as the team pointed out to the golf club the readings showed significant indicators that large lumps of ferrous metal were buried there.

Clearly, aircraft construction was primarily of aluminium alloy although that is not to say that that there were generally certain quantities of steel included in the airframe construction. For example; armour plating, engine internals and not least of all the landing gear. In this instance, the He 177 carried enormous double undercarriage legs on each wing. The latter assemblies were almost telegraph pole in size, and certainly comparable in diameter. So, the ferrous readings could well be coming from items such as this. On the other hand, the possibility could not be excluded that the readings were emanating from the steel casings of buried bombs. Whilst the site would not be disturbed by the building of the new road it did present a possible dilemma for the club. With knowledge that possibly, just possibly, there were unexploded bombs beneath the manicured greens, and right adjacent to what would be the main Hastings to London road, the club decided that some sort of action needed to be taken. The question was what? This was answered, at least in part, by a routine meeting between the club secretary and their insurance broker on 5 January 2004.

Clearly concerned by any liability issues that might arise, the broker insisted that the club had a duty to notify the authorities that a bomb (or bombs) might be buried there. Despite the fact that the site was not going to be disturbed by the road construction works the public had unrestricted access there, with golfers walking over the spot just about every day of the year. As a consequence of the broker's understandable concerns, the MOD were duly notified and an explosive ordnance disposal team detailed to survey the site. The task carried out, the results were not absolutely conclusive. Certainly there were readings, and these could certainly be bombs although in the event the EOD team advised that only disruptive excavations of the course would resolve the matter. Not only that, but the EOD experts advised that there was possibly greater risk in excavating and dealing with any bombs than in leaving them there. Given that the site was not in danger of disturbance the decision was taken to leave matters be. Whatever was there, including perhaps a missing man, would be staying there.

As regards the possibility of unexploded bombs being present, we have seen that the magnetometer readings might well have been caused by steel other than bomb casings. There are other contra-indicators, too, that might point away from bombs being present. First, official Luftwaffe reports indicate that this aircraft was hit and shot down on its return flight from London – in other words, after it had delivered its huge bomb load. On the other hand, the RAF intelligence report into the crash stated: "Aircraft was on fire in the air and crashed at a shallow angle. It is estimated that a least two large calibre bombs exploded on impact and the wreckage was completely destroyed. No information of interest could be obtained from the wreckage." So, the possibility exists that the aircraft did crash with its bomb load on board although, even if some had exploded, it was still possible that others remained intact in the wreckage. Such instances were not uncommon. On the other hand, the RAF crash investigators in 1944 could have been misled by the enormous crater. Perhaps this had merely been blasted in the soft Wealden clay by the impact of the huge crashing bomber, and not by bomb detonations at all? Maybe the impact points of the two enormous coupled aero engines had given the impressions of two bomb craters? Whatever the truth of the matter, the secret remains destined to lie permanently beneath ongoing games of golf. But what of the missing man?

If, as the 1944 report suggests, there were indeed explosions of two bombs then this might well have explained his disappearance. On the other hand, his disappearance could

Species: Fagus Sylvatica
In memory of Fx. Ernst Graff who lost his life
on 24 February 1944 aged 23.
The Heinkel 177 bomber in which he was shot
down lies beneath this surface.
May he rest in peace.
16 February 2005

The unaccounted-for man is Fw Ernst Graf whose last resting place is now remembered by Lamberhurst Golf Club who have erected this plaque (despite inaccuracies) in his memory.

equally be explained by his being buried with the wreckage of the He 177. Either way, here was the last resting place of that airman and the golf club decided that his passing should be marked. It was one of those acts that perhaps marked out the British soul that Heinz Möllenbrok had so eloquently described as epitomising fair play and human decency and saw a plaque to the memory of this missing Luftwaffe flier being placed at the base of a tree close to the eleventh tee. Whilst he may be missing, twenty-two-year-old Fw Ernst Graf is no longer forgotten.

Ernst Graf was one of the air gunners on board what was Heinkel He 177 A-3, coded 5J + PK, Werke Nummer 2222 of 2./KG 100 operating from its base at Rheine in Germany that had been flown by Oblt Wilhelm Hundt on the operation that night. The pilot, along with Uffz Rolf Luce (another of the gunners) had been killed and the pair were originally buried in the Lamberhurst Parish Churchyard of St Mary The Virgin. Subsequently, they have been moved to the Cannock Chase German Military Cemetery. Of the other crew, Uffz Wolfgang Michaelis (observer), Gefr Adolf Kreiser (radio operator) and Uffz Konrad Keusch (bomb aimer) were taken prisoner of war although which one of them was found shuffling along a Tunbridge Wells street by a sleepy policeman is unknown. If it was the bomb aimer then he would have held the key to knowing what was or was not still aboard his aircraft when he abandoned it.

Whilst the mystery of the He 177 at Lamberhurst golf course endures (at least in terms of knowing what lies beneath the turf), it can be said for certain that Ernst Graf met his end here. He has no headstone at Cannock, and no known grave. And yet his monument at Lamberhurst, set in the tranquil beauty of this glorious country golf course, seems fittingly appropriate. With scores of golfers passing by each and every day it is probably true to say that his name is seen and remembered by many more people than would otherwise be the case were he to be buried at Cannock Chase.

CHAPTER 17

German Burials in Wartime Britain

ALTHOUGH WE HAVE SEEN in previous chapters that Luftwaffe airmen who had been killed in action over the British Isles were not always afforded decent burial rites, it is certainly the case that the vast majority of those casualties were treated with respect and reverence. Indeed, it is also the case that such casualties were almost always given burials with full military honours; flag-draped coffins, honour parties, firing parties and buglers and a formal burial service conducted by a member of the clergy in accordance with normal Christian rites. Thereafter, the graves were marked by the Imperial War Graves Commission (forerunner of the Commonwealth War Graves Commission) with standard wooden markers bearing the name, rank, relevant arm of service and the date of death. The grave markers were duly photographed and copies of the photos were sent, via the Red Cross and Order of St John, to the next of kin in Germany or Austria in a small presentation folder. Not only that, but personal possessions such as rings, watches, badges, wallets etc were also routinely returned to the families via the Red Cross route after examination and recording by RAF air intelligence officers. Generally, all of the foregoing met the clear requirements laid down under the Geneva Convention for the treatment of enemy war dead:

> "Burial of the dead must be carried out individually if possible and must be preceded by a careful examination in order to confirm death and establish identity. The burials should be honourable and, if possible, according to the rites of the religion to which the deceased belonged. Graves must be properly maintained, with adequate record keeping, so that they may be found later."

Those, then, were the requirements imposed upon the British under that convention but let us first look at the process of interment for those German casualties who fell, or were found, the length and breadth of Britain and all around its extensive coastlines for the entire duration of the 1939-45 war. In total, this was a figure of somewhere in excess of 5,000 casualties, these comprising not only Luftwaffe aircrew but also deceased prisoners of war (including army and navy) and also including naval personnel washed up around Britain's shores.

Although some Luftwaffe airmen brought down over Britain were not afforded decent burial rites, most were buried with full military honours. Here, Lt Helmut Krüger and Ofw Wilhelm Stolle are laid to rest at St Margaret's Church, Catton, Norfolk. The two men were part of the crew of a Dornier 17 of 4./KG 3 shot down into the sea off Scolt Head on 21 August 1940, their bodies being washed ashore at Brancaster on 23 and 24 August respectively. Both casualties have now been moved to Cannock Chase German Military Cemetery. It is interesting to compare this elaborate burial ceremony with its swastika-draped coffins with the aftermath of the Junkers 88 shot down at King's Somborne which, coincidentally, was on the very same day as these two casualties – 21 August 1940.

When a casualty was found it fell to the responsibility of the local authority within whose boundaries he had died or been discovered to effect the burial of that casualty. Generally, this would be within the burial ground or churchyard of the district that was in use at that time for normal day-to-day burials. In the case of municipal cemeteries this was often in (or adjacent to) an established war graves plot although in many cases German burials were carried out in a remote corner away from the burial plots generally in use. Quite likely this was out of deference to local opinion and we do know that there was often open hostility from the local populace to burial of the enemy dead in their midst. Certainly, and as we have seen throughout this book, feelings had often run high and we only have to look at the case of the King's Somborne Junkers 88 crew to see that those feelings sometimes ran on long past the war's end. However, the casualties had to be decently buried somewhere and it fell to the respective local councils to see that this was done. In this respect, the councils were obliged to provide burial plots and cover all undertaking fees and settle the clergy fees etc. As for the burials themselves, these were almost always carried out by military personnel and usually (at least in the case of Luftwaffe personnel) by the nearest RAF unit.

When a Heinkel 111 of 4./KG 55 was shot down at Upper Frithfold Farm near Northchapel, West Sussex, on 16 August 1940 its crew of five were all killed although only one could be positively identified. He was Uffz Erich Schmidtke. Erich was buried in Ebernoe churchyard along with his four 'unknown' comrades. Later, when the German War Graves Service exhumed the remains for re-burial at Cannock Chase the four unknown men were identified and thus all five crew members now have named headstones.

APPENDIX I

Cannock Chase German Military Cemetery

POST-WAR THE QUESTION arose as to what should be done as regards to the continuing maintenance of the German war graves scattered the length and breadth of the country. The numbers involved, and the widely dispersed nature of the burials, meant that the cost and logistics of care and maintenance would become problematical in future years. In the years immediately after the war the temporary wooden markers fell into disrepair, inscriptions became illegible and the general upkeep of the graves was left to nature. In a few instances, the markers vanished completely whilst on the other hand some were lovingly cared for and tended by usually anonymous locals. However, something had to be done in the long term and whilst the Imperial War Graves Commission had initially discharged HM Government's obligation under the Geneva Convention to bury and mark the graves of enemy war dead, there was no ongoing obligation for the commission to look after them. Indeed, they neither had the resources nor mandate to do so. Something permanent had to be done for the future.

On 16 October 1959 an agreement was concluded by the government of the United Kingdom and the Federal Republic of Germany for the future care of the graves of German nationals who had lost their lives in the war of 1914-18 and 1939-45. This agreement provided for the transfer to a central cemetery in the United Kingdom of all graves which were not situated in cemeteries or plots already maintained by the Commonwealth War Graves Commission. In those cases, the German graves were left in situ under new stone grave markers and maintained on an agency basis by the commission. All other graves were to be removed under Home Office exhumation protocols and concentrated into the new German Military Cemetery for Britain which was to be located at Cannock Chase, Staffordshire, administered by the Volksbund Deutsche Kriegsgräberfürsorge (German War Graves Service). Consequently, and in order to implement the 1959 agreement, teams were dispatched during the early 1960s to the scatter of often isolated graveyards, municipal cemeteries and rural churchyards where the German war dead had been buried and were carefully exhumed for eventual re-burial.

It was very often the case that during this process of centralising the burials it became possible to identify casualties when they were exhumed and who had been buried as unknowns. Sometimes, details entered in burial registers provided the vital clues and

Reflection. Former Dornier 17-Z Battle of Britain pilot Heinz Möllenbrok at the Cannock Chase German Military Cemetery. Two of his crewmen when he was shot down on 16 August 1940 are buried here, as are many former members of his old unit, KG2.

othertimes this was through the discovery of identity discs or effects that had been missed during the original burial. On other occasions it was uniform rank markings, dental records or other official information such as the height and ages of casualties which enabled previously unidentified men to be named through a process of elimination if not by absolute proof.

A case in point is that of Ofw Oskar Strack of 1./JG 52 who had been lost over southern England on 26 October 1940. For many years it had been assumed by researchers that the unknown airman buried at Tunbridge Wells, Kent, and who had been killed in the crash of a Messerschmitt 109 at Chalket Farm, Pembury, was probably Uffz Geiswinkler of 6./JG 53 who had been lost on the same day as Strack. In fact, it transpired that when this unknown airman had been exhumed during the 1960s for re-burial at Cannock Chase a tobacco tin had been found with the body. On it was inscribed O.St, sufficient evidence of identification for the German authorities to declare that this man was in fact Oskar Strack and thereby to close yet another missing airman case.

In one or two cases, although not many, next of kin elected to have the casualty returned home for burial in family graves but by the late 1960s the whole process had been concluded with the burials that were to be left in situ identified and those graves permanently marked and the others removed for re-burial at Cannock.

The site at Cannock, which had been carefully chosen, is in a particularly beautiful location. Situated alongside the A34 road from Walsall to Stafford, the land falls away from the access road at the south side to a natural valley running from south west to north east and, beyond, the land rises up again to the open heather-covered chaseland which lies on the east side of the main road. There are numerous clumps of mature silver birch trees across the site that add to the natural beauty of the cemetery and the headstones were designed to stand in beds of purple heather and other plants indigenous to Cannock Chase. The graves are collectively set in groups with each group set in large rectangular beds of heather. The actual headstones, including one small set of horizontal ones, are of dark grey Belgian stone and each upright marker bears the names of four men with their rank and dates of birth and death.

The burials follow the convention of equality in death with each name and headstone of uniform design and pattern. No special recognition or privilege is afforded those of senior rank and neither is there any indication of any award of gallantry. Thus, a highly decorated general might easily lie side-by-side with a lowly corporal. Elsewhere on the site, an elevated terrace contains the communal graves of four Zeppelin crews who were shot down over England during the First World War. These four graves are each marked by four massive stone slabs with a large commemorative stone tablet alongside. In the centre of the cemetery stands a simple thirty-five-foot-high cross of smooth-faced concrete.

A group of buildings at the entrance to the cemetery includes a List Room where a register of all burials is maintained and where a huge acid-etched glass panel marks out the cemetery plan. Adjacent is the Hall of Honour with its centrepiece bronze of a fallen warrior by German sculptor, Professor Hans Wimmer.

Despite its strange beauty, there is perhaps a sombre aspect to this cemetery. Unlike the Lutyens-designed or inspired cemeteries of the Commonwealth War Graves Commission, and where a certain sense of triumph and victory over so many deaths suffered in a noble cause quite tangibly pervades, this German cemetery perhaps reflects something of the dark shadow which falls over the cause for which these men lost their lives. That said, it is surely fitting and appropriate that these comrades-in-arms now lie together in peace and in the tranquil countryside of the land they came to conquer and in a place visited often by respectful citizens who would have once been their enemies.

Whilst records of the burials concentrated at Cannock (approximately 4,929 in total) are held in the List Room, there is no listing of those casualties who died in attacks against the British Isles and for whom there is no known grave. Unlike the British and Americans, no such published or memorialised centralised listing exists and it is quite simply the case that if a German serviceman is missing he remains un-commemorated. There is no listing, for example, like that on the Runnymede Memorial or that found on The Wall of The Missing at Madingley American Military Cemetery in Cambridgeshire. Drawing up any such listing would be a virtually impossible task for German losses. However, and in an attempt to redress this gap in official listing and commemoration, and to give some balance to the fact that in *Finding The Few*, the companion volume to this book, a listing of all missing RAF aircrew during the Battle of Britain is carried, so a similar listing follows at Appendix II for

Luftwaffe aircrew missing during operations against the British Isles during the roughly comparable time frame.

NOTE: Readers wishing to carry out their own research into German casualties, or who seek details of casualties buried at Cannock Chase (or elsewhere) may find the following contact details for the German War Graves Service useful:-

Volksbund Deutsche Kriegsgräberfürsorge
Werner-Hilpert Straße 2
34112 Kassel
Germany
Website: www.volksbund.de

NB: The author would be pleased to receive information, photographs, eyewitness accounts etc in relation to the various incidents and casualties contained within this book, or to hear from anyone with additional information in relation to other cases not listed here. He may be contacted via the publishers, Grub Street, at 4 Rainham Close, London, SW11 6SS, e-mail milhis@grubstreet.co.uk

APPENDIX II

Luftwaffe Airmen Missing over Britain 10 July to 31 October 1940

One of the first Luftwaffe 'missing' casualties during the official period of the Battle of Britain was Oblt Hans-Joachim Göring (left), nephew of Reichsmarschall Hermann Göring, killed when his Messerschmitt 110 was shot down at Portland on 11 July 1940. No trace of him or of his comrade, Uffz Zimmerman, was ever found.

12 July	Me 110	9./ZG 76	Oblt H-J Göring Uffz A Zimmerman	Portland, Dorset
12 Aug	Ju 88	8./KG 51	Uffz K Rösch	Portsmouth Harbour, Hants
13 Aug	Do 17	8./KG 2	Oblt W Morich Oblt G Müller	Seasalter, Kent

Although no trace of Oblt Josef Oestermann could be found when his Junkers 88 slammed into the ground at Philliswood, Treyford, in West Sussex (inset) on 13 August 1940 a memorial to his memory has since been erected at the crash site.

13 Aug	Ju 88	Stab I/KG 54	Oblt J Oestermann	Treyford, West Sussex
15 Aug	Ju 88	4./KG 30	Uffz A Neumeyer	Hunmanby, Yorkshire
15 Aug	Ju 88	5./LG 1	Fw H Pauck Uffz K Glitzner Fw D Rugge Uffz E Woldt	West Tisted, Hants
16 Aug	Do 17	7./KG 76	Ofw E Riedel Ofw E Brauer	Paddock Wood, Kent
16 Aug	Do 17	3./KG 2	Oblt H-J Brandenburg Gefr K Hirsch Gefr E Genter Flgr H Koch	Whitstable Beach, Kent
16 Aug	Me 110	5./ZG 76	Obgefr J Lewandowski	Shopwyke, West Sussex
18 Aug	Me 109	III./JG 3	Lt E von Fonderen	Bredhurst, Kent
18 Aug	Ju 87	3./StG 77	Oblt D Lehmann Uffz H Winiarski	Chidham, West Sussex

18 Aug	Me 110	1./ZG 26	Uffz R Mai Uffz J Gebauer	Harbledown, Kent
18 Aug	Me 110	3./ZG 26	Ofw W Stange Uffz H Hesse	Bonnington, Kent
18 Aug	Me 110	4./ZG 26	Hptm H Lütke Uffz H Brillo	Clacton, Essex
18 Aug	Me 110	6./ZG 26	Oblt H Hellmuth Fw F Winter	Platts Heath, Kent
21 Aug	Ju 88	1./KG 54	Oblt M-D Birkenstock Obgefr G Freude Uffz R Schulze Gefr F Becker	King's Somborne, Hants
25 Aug	Me 110	8./ZG 76	Fw M Dähne Obgefr F Müller	Buckland Ripers, Dorset
3 Sept	Do 17	5./KG 2	Lt H Schildt Uffz E Swindek Gefr P Niegisch	Langenhoe, Essex

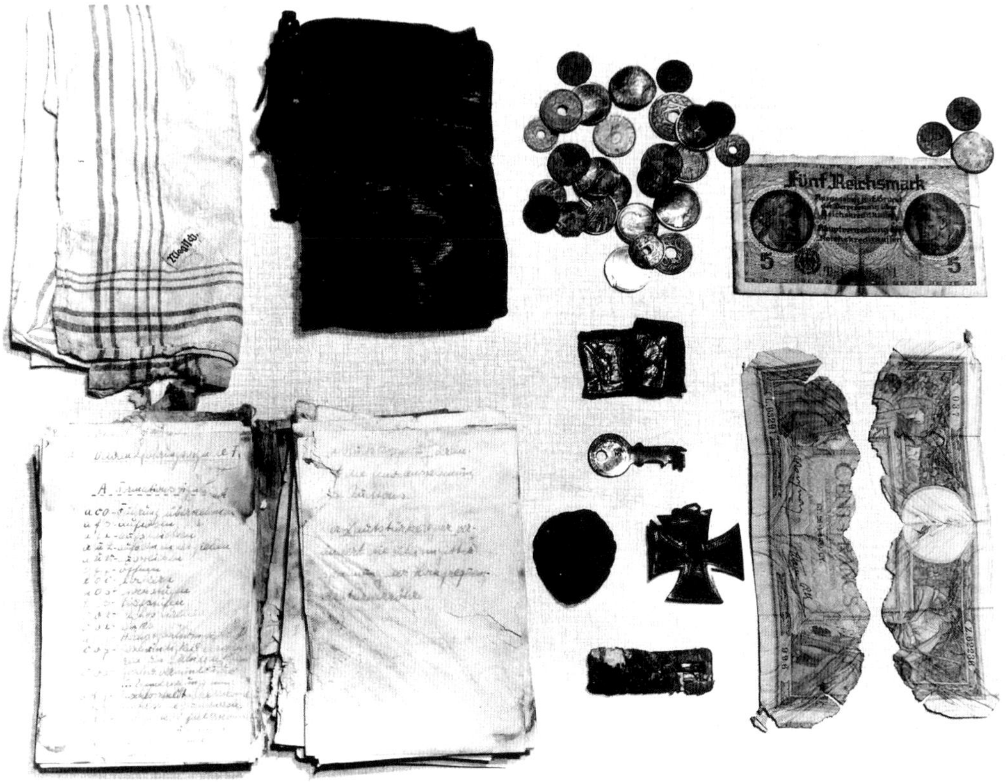

Three crew members of a KG 2 Dornier 17 were missing after the crash of their aircraft at Langenhoe, Essex. Although no tangible remains were reported when the site was excavated by the London Air Museum in the 1970s, a whole range of personal effects told their own story. Included in the finds were an Iron Cross, a wound badge, notebook and a handkerchief clearly marked with the name of one of the crew, Gefr Niegisch.

One of the first 'aviation archaeology' digs was conducted by Battle of Britain historians Peter Foote and Dennis Knight on the crash site of a Messerschmitt 110 at Church Farm, Washington. In 1940 an RAF intelligence officer had noted the aircraft number (2837) thus confirming this to be the Me 110 lost on 4 September with Oblt Florenz and Gefr Herbert who are both unaccounted for. Evidence that both men were still in the wreckage was discovered, including coins and a Luftwaffe belt buckle. However, not long after these investigations the construction of the A24 road sliced straight through the crash site and today traffic thunders over what had been the last resting place of Florenz and Herbert. Here, Dennis Knight examines one of the dinghy paddles during the 1965 excavation.

4 Sept	Me 110	Stab III./ZG 76	Oblt H Florenz Gefr R Herbert	Washington, West Sussex
5 Sept	Me 109	7./JG 53	Lt J Deutsch	Eastchurch, Essex
6 Sept	Me 110	1./ErpGr 210	Uffz G Rüger	Crowhurst, Surrey
6 Sept	Me 109	7./JG 26	Gefr K-G A Holzapfel	Old Romney, Kent
8 Sept	Do 17	5./KG 2	Uffz H Flick Uffz W Trost Uffz W Selter	Leeds, Kent
11 Sept	Me 110	9./ZG 26	Oblt J Junghans Gefr P Eckert	Harvel, Kent
15 Sept	Do 17	5./KG 3	Oblt H Becker-Ross Ofw G Brückner Fw A Hansen Fw W Brinkmann	Marden, Kent
18 Sept	Me 109	1./JG 27	Oblt R Krafftschick	Stockbury, Kent
18 Sept	Ju 88	8./KG 77	Ofw W Semerau Uffz H Treutmann	Harty, Kent
20 Sept	Me 109	9./JG 27	Uffz E Clauser	Ospringe, Kent
20 Sept	Ju 88	4./KG 54	Ofw M Röhrig Fw H Fischer Gefr K Neumann	Merton, Surrey
27 Sept	Ju 88	3./KG 77	Uffz M Merschen	Horsmonden, Kent
27 Sept	Ju 88	Stab II./KG 77	Oblt K-H Lutze	Penshurst, Kent
1 Oct	Me 109	4./JG 26	Uffz H Bluder	Falmer, East Sussex
8 Oct	He 111	8./KG 55	Lt U Flügge Uffz J Ehrensberger Uffz E Herber Gefr H Pawlik	Rowlands Castle, Hants
27 Oct	Do 17	7./KG 26	Uffz E Johannes	Holbrook Creek, Essex

NOTE: The criteria for inclusion in this table is that the airmen shown are all missing and do not have known graves. All of the casualties were lost between 10 July and 31 October 1940, a period later recognised by the British as the accepted span of the Battle of Britain. All of those listed are either known or believed to have fallen on land within the British Isles or else in harbours or inland estuaries. No attempt has been made to include the hundreds of such casualties known to have fallen just offshore from the British coast. In the case of the above listing, the location of the incident is shown in the right-hand column. In some cases the airmen listed do not comprise complete crews of the aircraft involved; in many instances the other crew members will have escaped or else were otherwise accounted for. For reasons of space and clarity only the main type designation of the aircraft is shown and any sub-type is not included. (eg Do 17 rather than Do 17Z or Me 110 instead of Me 110 C-4 etc)

In the case of losses where crew names cannot be linked to the incident then these are not included – eg the Messerschmitt 110 at Slackstead Farm, Hursley, on 15 August 1940.

This listing is not necessarily exhaustive. It does not include those casualties detailed in this book who are no longer unaccounted for.

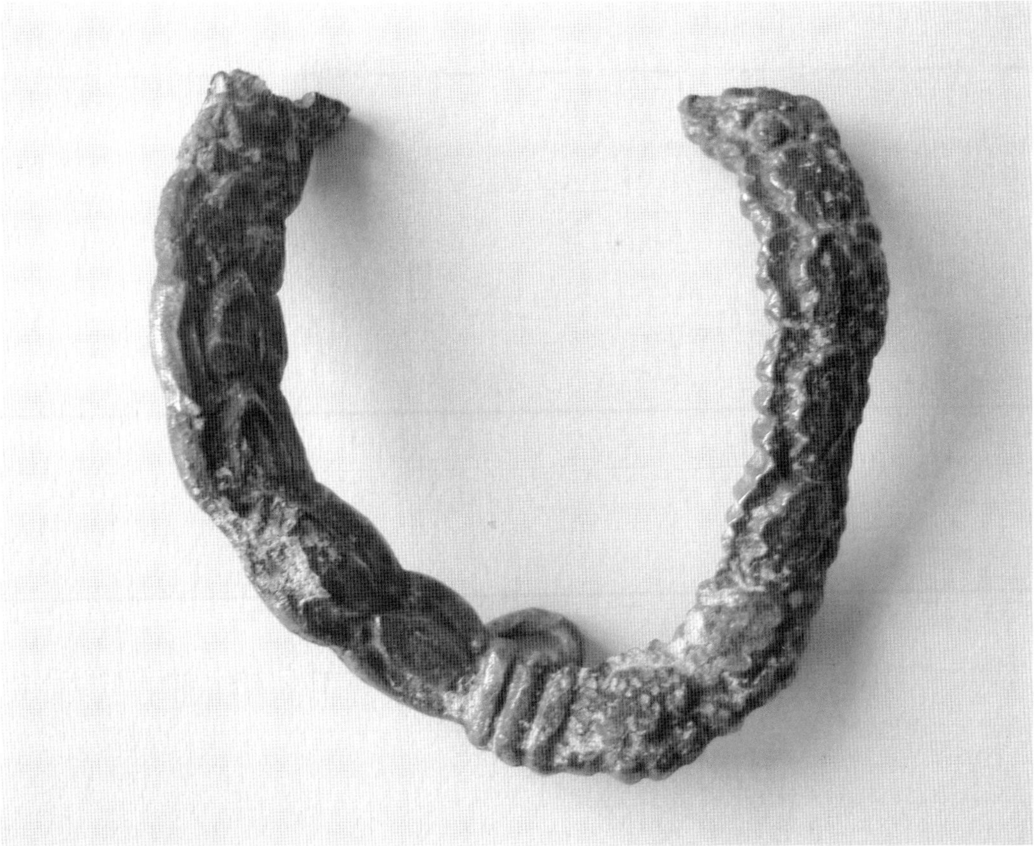

Although no excavations have taken place there, it must be assumed that the crash site of a 3./KG 77 Junkers 88 at Horsmonden, Kent, is the last resting place of its pilot, Uffz Merschen, who was never found. However, an item that can be connected directly to Matthias Merschen was discovered in the 1980s when this part of his Luftwaffe pilot's badge laurel wreath surround was picked up there. Presumably Merschen's remains must lay somewhere nearby. This small item, a tangible link to 1940, somehow sums up the sad stories of those men covered in this book who simply disappeared and who have no known grave.

Selected Bibliography

The following books and publications were referred to by the author during the preparation of this work.

Bungay, Stephen	*The Most Dangerous Enemy*	(Aurum 2001)
Forell, Fritz von	*Mölders und Seine Männner*	(Steirische Verlagsanstalt Graz 1941)
Goss, Chris	*Luftwaffe Fighters Battle of Britain*	(Crécy 2000)
Goss, Chris	*Luftwaffe Bombers Battle of Britain*	(Crécy 2000)
Goss, Chris	*Brothers in Arms*	(Crécy 1994)
Mason, Frank	*Battle Over Britain*	(McWhirter Twins 1969)
Obermaier, Ernst	*Die Ritterkreuztrager Band 1*	(Verlag Dieter Hoffmann 1970)
Parry, Simon W	*Intruders Over Britain*	(Air Research 1987)
Ramsey, Winston G	*Battle of Britain Then And Now*	(After The Battle 1980)
Ramsey, Winston G	*Blitz Then And Now (Vol.1)*	(After The Battle 1987)
Ramsey, Winston G	*Blitz Then And Now (Vol.2)*	(After The Battle 1987)
Ramsey, Winston G	*Blitz Then And Now (Vol.3)*	(After The Battle 1987)
Reis, Karl Jr	*Markings & Camouflage Sytems Of Luftwaffe Aircraft in WW2*	(Verlag Dieter Hoffman 1971)
Smith, Peter C	*Luftwaffe Ju 87 Dive Bomber Units*	(Classic 2006)
Smith, Peter C	*Stuka Squadron*	(PSL 1990)
Smith, Richard J and Creek, Eddie	*Heinkel He 177 Greif*	(Classic 2008)
Vasco, John J and Cornwell, Peter D	*Zerstörer*	(JAC 1995)
Von Eimannsberger, Ludwig	*Zerstörer Gruppe*	(Schiffer 1998)
Weal, John	*JG 51 Mölders*	(Osprey 2006)
Wood, Derek and Dempster, Derek	*The Narrow Margin*	(Arrow Books 1969)
Wynn, Kenneth	*Men of The Battle of Britain*	(CCB 2000)
Zeng L, Stankey D G, with Creek E	*Bomber Units of The Luftwaffe*	(Midland 2007)
Ziegler, Frank H	*The Story of 609 Squadron*	(Macdonald 1971)

Index

People

Places

Airfields

RAF Squadrons

Luftwaffe Staffeln

Gruppen